SpringerBriefs in Psychology

SpringerBriefs present concise summaries of cutting-edge research and practical applications across a wide spectrum of fields. Featuring compact volumes of 50 to 125 pages, the series covers a range of content from professional to academic. Typical topics might include:

- A timely report of state-of-the-art analytical techniques
- A bridge between new research results as published in journal articles and a contextual literature review
- A snapshot of a hot or emerging topic
- An in-depth case study or clinical example
- A presentation of core concepts that readers must understand to make independent contributions

SpringerBriefs in Psychology showcase emerging theory, empirical research, and practical application in a wide variety of topics in psychology and related fields. Briefs are characterized by fast, global electronic dissemination, standard publishing contracts, standardized manuscript preparation and formatting guidelines, and expedited production schedules.

More information about this series at https://link.springer.com/bookseries/10143

Stefan T. Güntert • Theo Wehner • Harald A. Mieg

Organizational, Motivational, and Cultural Contexts of Volunteering

The European View

 Springer

Stefan T. Güntert
FHNW
University of Applied Sciences and Arts
Northwestern Switzerland
Basel, Switzerland

Theo Wehner
Swiss Federal Institute of Technology
Zurich, Switzerland

Harald A. Mieg
Humboldt-Universität zu Berlin
Berlin, Germany

ISSN 2192-8363　　　　　　　　　ISSN 2192-8371　(electronic)
SpringerBriefs in Psychology
ISBN 978-3-030-92819-3　　　　　ISBN 978-3-030-92817-9　(eBook)
https://doi.org/10.1007/978-3-030-92817-9

© The Author(s) 2022. This book is an open access publication.

Open Access This book is licensed under the terms of the Creative Commons Attribution 4.0 International License (http://creativecommons.org/licenses/by/4.0/), which permits use, sharing, adaptation, distribution and reproduction in any medium or format, as long as you give appropriate credit to the original author(s) and the source, provide a link to the Creative Commons license and indicate if changes were made.

The images or other third party material in this book are included in the book's Creative Commons license, unless indicated otherwise in a credit line to the material. If material is not included in the book's Creative Commons license and your intended use is not permitted by statutory regulation or exceeds the permitted use, you will need to obtain permission directly from the copyright holder.

The use of general descriptive names, registered names, trademarks, service marks, etc. in this publication does not imply, even in the absence of a specific statement, that such names are exempt from the relevant protective laws and regulations and therefore free for general use.

The publisher, the authors and the editors are safe to assume that the advice and information in this book are believed to be true and accurate at the date of publication. Neither the publisher nor the authors or the editors give a warranty, expressed or implied, with respect to the material contained herein or for any errors or omissions that may have been made. The publisher remains neutral with regard to jurisdictional claims in published maps and institutional affiliations.

This Springer imprint is published by the registered company Springer Nature Switzerland AG
The registered company address is: Gewerbestrasse 11, 6330 Cham, Switzerland

Preface

Few communities can exist without the unpaid activities of volunteers. The care of the elderly or disabled, the commitment to environmental protection and nature conservation, the activities of election workers or lay assessors, honorary positions in communities, sports clubs, and churches; all these tasks and functions are in fact dependent on volunteers. How can we understand voluntary work? How essential is it for this kind of work to remain unpaid and to be carried out by so-called laypersons with special motives? And what follows from this for the interaction between voluntary work and professionalized, paid employment? These are the questions we address with this book on volunteer work.

This book offers a *comprehensive view of the phenomenon of volunteer work:* it combines motivational questions with questions of corporate organization and the social environment. In particular, it is the first book to present volunteer work in detail as a psychosocial resource, a source of well-being that should not be overused or abused. This book is a clear instruction on how to design volunteer work tasks and where boundaries must be respected (i.e., not straying into "illegitimate" tasks that exceed the goodwill and/or competences of the volunteer community). It is based on 15 years of research into volunteer work in Europe. It offers an insight into cultural and national differences and provides concrete advice for the organization of volunteer work.

We will show that: Volunteering fulfills many functions—for the individual and for the community. This finding is well documented empirically through both quantitative data and interviews. However, the ways in which the various functions are distributed or shift over time and how they are related to the given political, organizational, social, and individual framework conditions is something that requires nationwide volunteer reports on the one hand and hypothesis-driven research on the other—those are the questions that this book reports on. We will argue from an occupational and organizational psychological perspective and also refer to gainful employment. Even though psychological research on volunteering is not very well developed, the available findings are considerable:

- The motives of volunteers are multifunctional, and the various functions (learning, social interaction, value reference, etc.) change during the course of the commitment. Volunteering at an older age fulfills a balancing function to professional life.
- While in gainful employment, the holistic nature and variety of tasks are central; similarly, autonomy and the meaningfulness of the activity are important to volunteers.
- Even if it can be assumed that healthy, socially competent, and secure individuals are more likely to volunteer, it can be shown that volunteering keeps people healthy: Volunteering keeps people healthy, promises recognition, and serves to fulfill meaning.

Zurich, Switzerland Stefan Güntert
May 2021 Theo Wehner
Harald A. Mieg

Acknowledgments

This book is largely based on the work of Wehner and Güntert (2015). Specific text contributions come from Susanne Freund (Chap. 3), Hanna Ketterer (Chap. 5), Anja Lehmann (Chap. 1), Max Neufeind (Chap. 5), Romualdo Ramos (Chap. 4), and Susan van Schie (Chap. 3 & 6). Funding for this book was provided by the Swiss Federal Institute of Technology, Zurich, and the Schweizerische Gemeinnützige Gesellschaft (Swiss Society for the Common Good).

The core results and findings on volunteering work presented are based on the work of the research group at the Swiss Federal Institute of Technology, Zurich, led from 2004 to 2014 by Theo Wehner. This team included:

THEO WEHNER, Swiss Federal Institute of Technology Zurich, Switzerland

REBECCA BRAUCHLI, ZHAW—Zurich University of Applied Sciences, Winterthur, Switzerland

MICHAEL DICK, Otto-von-Guericke-Universität Magdeburg, Germany

SUSANNE FREUND, Katholische Universität Eichstätt-Ingolstadt, Germany

GIAN-CLAUDIO GENTILE, AXA, Winterthur, Switzerland

STEFAN GÜNTERT, FHNW University of Applied Sciences, Basel, Switzerland

JULIA S. HUMM, Zurich, Switzerland

PATRICK JIRANEK, Swiss Federal Institute of Technology Zurich, Switzerland

ELISABETH KALS, Katholische Universität Eichstätt-Ingolstadt, Germany

HANNA KETTERER, Friedrich- Schiller-Universität Jena, Germany

HARALD A. MIEG, Humboldt-Universität zu Berlin, Germany

GINA MÖSKEN, The German Children and Youth Foundation, Magdeburg, Germany

MAX NEUFEIND, Federal Ministry of Finance, Berlin, Germany

JEANNETTE OOSTLANDER, Schaffhausen, Switzerland

ROMUALDO F. RAMOS, Medical University of Vienna, Austria

ISABEL T. STRUBEL, Katholische Universität Eichstätt-Ingolstadt, Germany

MATTHIAS WÄCHTER, Hochschule Luzern, Lucerne, Switzerland

SUSAN VAN SCHIE, Jiva Development GmbH, Zurich, Switzerland

Contents

1 **Definition of Volunteer Work and a Model of Volunteer Activity** 1
   1.1 Introduction: A Clarification of Terms 1
   1.2 Volunteering in Europe: Statistics, Trends 2
      1.2.1 Trends in Germany, Austria, and Switzerland: From Formal to Informal Volunteering, Shorter Duration of Commitment, but Minor Changes in Gender Distribution 3
      1.2.2 Persistent Inequalities: Income and Education 4
      1.2.3 Volunteering Fulfills Many Functions: Wanting to Make a Difference "In a Small Way" 5
   1.3 Volunteer Work as a Meaningful Activity 6
   1.4 The Voluntary Engagement of Older People 8
   References 9

2 **Volunteer Work as a Matter of Motivation** 11
   2.1 The Functional Approach 11
   2.2 Extensions of the Functional Approach 12
   2.3 A Self-Determination Theory Perspective on Volunteer Motives 13
   References 17

3 **Volunteer Work as an Organizational Task** 19
   3.1 Volunteering as a Process 19
   3.2 Three Basic Psychological Needs as Orientation 20
   3.3 Neglected Importance of Tasks and Organization 21
   3.4 The Successful Design of Volunteer Work: An Empirical Study 23
      3.4.1 The Findings for the Task Characteristics 24

		3.4.2 Findings on Organizational Characteristics	25
		3.4.3 Findings on the Indicators of Sustained Engagement	26
	References		28
4	**Volunteering as a Psychosocial Resource**		**31**
	4.1	The Salutogenic Approach to Volunteering and Health	31
	4.2	The Interaction Between Paid Work and Volunteering	34
	4.3	Work–Life Balance	35
	4.4	Event Volunteering, Voluntourism	36
	References		40
5	**Volunteer Work from an International Perspective**		**45**
	5.1	Structural Approaches	46
		5.1.1 Social Welfare and Altruistic Motivation	46
		5.1.2 Signal Value and Career Motivation	46
	5.2	Cultural Approaches	47
		5.2.1 Egalitarianism and Altruistic Motive	48
		5.2.2 Individualism and Career Motive	48
		5.2.3 Conservatism and the Motive of Social Adaptation	49
		5.2.4 Affective Autonomy and Protective Motive	49
		5.2.5 Intellectual Autonomy and Motive for Understanding	49
	5.3	Cultural and Structural Differences: Volunteer Work at the Red Cross in Europe	52
		5.3.1 Same Language, Similar Motives	55
		5.3.2 Volunteers in Non-Profit Organizations	55
	References		57
6	**Practical Implications**		**61**
	6.1	Which Design Features Influence Sustained Engagement?	61
		6.1.1 General Satisfaction	61
		6.1.2 Joy of Work	62
		6.1.3 Identification with the Organization	62
		6.1.4 Organizational Commitment	62
	6.2	Summary from the Perspective of Industrial and Organizational Psychology, with Recommendations for Action	63
	References		64

Chapter 1
Definition of Volunteer Work and a Model of Volunteer Activity

Volunteer work can best be defined as a free, non-profit activity that usually serves the common good. The aspect of *voluntariness* is essential and distinguishes it from other forms of work. Anyone who speaks of volunteer work is not just talking about individual helping behavior or civic engagement but, indirectly, always also about the national system of gainful employment within which volunteer work takes place and with which it must be compatible.

1.1 Introduction: A Clarification of Terms

We propose a reference definition that can be adopted, modified, or extended depending on the emphasis of the research topic or practical use (Mieg & Wehner, 2002):

> *Volunteer work* refers to non-profit activity including unpaid, self-organized or institutionally organized, socially oriented work; this means a *personal, non-profit* commitment that is connected with a regular, project- or event-related *expenditure of time*, which could in principle also be carried out by another person and *could potentially also be paid for*.

This definition refers to three essential characteristics of volunteer work, which should also be taken into account by research:

1. *Voluntariness*: The activity is free, autonomous, independent. From this follows: The coordination of volunteer work with gainful employment is not trivial; this coordination cannot be based solely on the logic of volunteer work.
2. *Non-profit status*: Volunteer work constitutes a not-for-profit system that adds value to society. A central question here is: How can this type of service and its added value—e.g., as social capital—be grasped without merely thinking about monetarization?

3. *Meaningful activity*: Voluntary work is a meaningful activity, whereby the question must be asked: What are the underlying motives? What can we learn, from volunteer work, for work in general and for the system of gainful employment in particular?

The term "non-profit" is used analogously to non-profit organizations and foundations to emphasize the contribution to the common good. We will use the reference definition in those places where we want to emphasize the special characteristics of voluntary work. Otherwise, we will also refer to them as "voluntary work" or "volunteering." However, volunteering is not the same as *lay work*: Many experts and professionals also undertake voluntary work within their field of expertise; moreover, volunteers can develop *expertise* for their work (cf. Mieg, 2001).

1.2 Volunteering in Europe: Statistics, Trends

We assume that voluntary work says something not only about individual helping behavior in the respective civil society within which it takes place, but—because of the aspect of work—is also closely related to the respective constitution of the national system of gainful employment. Thus, one can ask:

- Is volunteer work *neutral* and only secondary to gainful employment? The area of volunteer work then defines a parallel world to gainful employment and is to be understood similarly to the area of value-oriented religious practice or many balance-oriented hobbies.
- Is volunteer work *complementary* or even *compensatory* to gainful employment? Voluntary work would then offer room for motives and fulfillment of meaning that might not be provided by gainful employment.
- The function can also be *instrumental*: Voluntary work might also serve gainful employment, e.g., if biographically or professionally relevant qualifications and skills are to be acquired through voluntary work.
- It is conceivable that volunteer work is to be understood in a *recompensatory* way to gainful employment: Some people are so satisfied with and grateful for their work (and their lives) that they want to give something back to society through voluntary work.
- It is also conceivable that the relationship between voluntary work and gainful employment may be *conflictual*, at least at times, whether because time commitments cannot be mutually agreed upon or even that ideological rifts might emerge, for example, if an employee in the chemical industry also volunteered for Greenpeace.

In the following, we summarize the most important findings of the European Quality of Life Survey (EQLS).

The most recent EQLS survey of 2016 interviewed around 37,000 people "face-to-face" in the 33 European states (28 EU member States and five candidate

1.2 Volunteering in Europe: Statistics, Trends

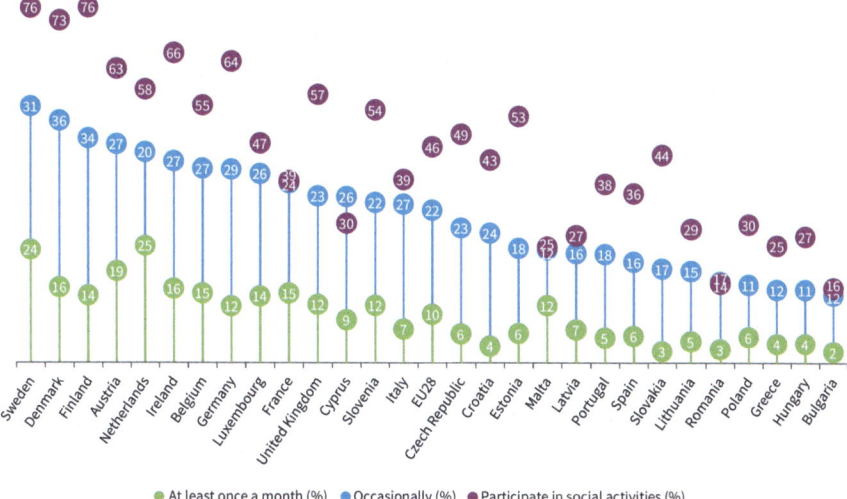

Fig. 1.1 Voluntary work in European countries (Eurofound, 2017, Fig. 34)

countries). The survey report devotes a separate chapter to voluntary work and organized social activities (Eurofound, 2017). Although the numbers of people involved in voluntary work (see Fig. 1.1) vary greatly, the average is impressive: *One in three EU citizens* (33%) carried out some voluntary work during the previous 12 months—similar to that for 2011. Rates of volunteering range from 6% in political parties or trade unions to 19% in educational, cultural, sports, or professional organizations (op.cit., p. 94).

With regard to the social profile of volunteers, the picture that has been familiar in the literature for many years is evident: Rates of volunteering are in fact higher among the *employed* than among the unemployed in the EU as a whole—and consistently so at country level. Higher volunteering rates, whether occasional or regular, are also associated with a higher *level of educational attainment* and *higher income* (p. 95).

1.2.1 Trends in Germany, Austria, and Switzerland: From Formal to Informal Volunteering, Shorter Duration of Commitment, but Minor Changes in Gender Distribution

Germany, Austria, and Switzerland produce volunteer surveys based on population-representative *telephone interviews*. In Germany, the surveys (approximately 38,000 participants) have been conducted every five years since 1999. All findings reported here are from 2019 (see BMFSFJ, 2021). For Switzerland, data from the fourth wave of the survey (about 5000 interviews) are available from 2019 (see Lamprecht et al., 2020); for Austria, from the third wave (about 4000 interviews) and the survey year 2016 (see BMASK, 2016). The three—predominantly German-speaking—countries have particular specifics but are nevertheless compared here, given their similarly pronounced engagement rates and survey instruments. *Germany* is one of the largest EU countries, with a resident population of about 83 million, of which about 14% are non-German citizens. *Austria* is home to around 8.6 million people, of which foreigners make up about 16%. *Switzerland*, which is not part of the EU and has three language regions, has a population of around 8.5 million, with foreigners making up around 25%.

In all three countries, a distinction is made between *formal volunteering* (carried out in associations and organizations) and *informal volunteering* (self-organized and carried out outside the home). The Swiss data reveal a trend that is also evident to a lesser extent in the other surveys: A shift in engagement (of 6%) from the formal to the informal sector. For the 55 to 74 age group, the ratio is 44%:52% (formal: informal) and even rises to 77% for informal neighborhood help for this age group (see: www.beisheim-stiftung.com). In the report from Germany, this observation reads as follows: "More and more committed people carry out their activities in informally organized frameworks, which generally have flatter hierarchical structures and require fewer management and board positions" (BMFSFJ, 2021, p. 40).

In Germany, approximately 17% of volunteers spent six or more hours per week on their commitment in 2019. Since 1999, there has been *a trend toward less time-intensive volunteering*: The proportion of volunteers who invest a lot of time in their volunteering activities (six or more hours per week) fell by 6%, while the proportion of those who invest significantly less time (up to two hours per week) rose by 9% over the same period. The same trend can be seen in Austria and Switzerland.

In connection with the participation rate, the *gender distribution* is also interesting. Whereas in Germany, the first four waves (from 1999 to 2014) consistently showed higher engagement among men (in 1999, the difference was 10%), in 2019, there is no longer a statistically significant difference, this also being true for the other two countries. Furthermore, in all three countries, *women are more involved in the informal sector,* and men are more involved in the formal sector, with differences of between five and seven percent. Ultimately, these differences in distribution reflect the classic, rather conservative division of roles.

1.2.2 Persistent Inequalities: Income and Education

Differences in volunteering are evident—in all volunteer surveys known to us—not only in gender distribution, but also in age groups, between rural and urban populations, employment status, occupational status, and household income or form. To put it in a nutshell: *the more well-off individuals are, the higher the participation rate*. This is particularly evident for educational attainment (which is supportive for voluntary work) and, nowadays, migration background (less supportive).

As an example, the difference between persons with the highest and lowest *educational attainment* given for selection is a full 25% in Germany for the survey year 2019 (high education = 51%, low education = 26%). While in Austria in 2016, persons with compulsory education volunteered at 21%. Many experts and professionals also undertake voluntary work within their field of expertise. This unequal participation rate is additionally evident for the two sectors: Fewer people with only compulsory basic education are engaged in the formal sector. This means for participation rates in the formal sector for Switzerland in 2019: people with low educational attainment: 21%, with high educational attainment: 40%. In the informal sector, the ratio is 32% vs. 44%.

1.2.3 Volunteering Fulfills Many Functions: Wanting to Make a Difference "In a Small Way"

From the beginnings of psychological research on volunteers to the present day, the question of volunteers' motivations, attitudes, and motives has been and remains central. No volunteer survey, therefore, refrains from also asking about motivations for getting involved. The motivation has changed little over the last 10 years or more: *Fun* is high on the list, which, however, should be more aptly described as "enjoyment of the respective voluntary activity;" this is at least confirmed by self-reporting and qualitative interview data (see Wehner & Güntert, 2015). Consistently across all three countries, the three primary reasons are the desire: (1) to get together with other people, (2) to help or to do something useful: *Wanting to make a difference "in a small way."*

The fact that volunteering or helping one's neighbors might also benefit one's professional life is a relevant consideration for just under a quarter of volunteers in Austria in 2016. Sixteen percent of those involved also expect their unpaid commitment to help them enter a profession or paid employment. Whereas in 2006, only one in 12 people expected to benefit from volunteering when starting a career, by 2016, this proportion had risen to one in five. This is a trend that has also been evident in other volunteer surveys in recent years (see Freitag et al., 2016; Simonson et al., 2017; Stadelmann et al., 2010): In the working society, volunteering is becoming increasingly *relevant for career biographies* and is now also frequently listed in the curriculum vitae. As we can see, the boundaries between work and non-work are shifting, and this has implications for civic engagement, neighborhood help, and voluntary association activities (see Rosenkranz & Görtler, 2002).

1.3 Volunteer Work as a Meaningful Activity

We understand volunteer work as a meaningful activity. There is now a wealth of research on the concept of *meaningful work*. The approaches lead back to ideas that shaped science at the beginning of the twentieth century. On the one hand, the Russian activity theory (Aleksei N. Leont'ev)[1] and its social-cultural view (Lev S. Vygotski); on the other hand, the phenomenological thinking in German philosophy and sociology (e.g., Alfred Schütz, Hannah Arendt) with Arendt's plea for a "*vita activa*" as a legacy (Arendt, 1958: *The Human Condition*): Only in deliberate social practice, i.e., *vita activa*) can we do justice and dignity to ourselves and the human condition at the same time. In the context of this book, we should add that meaningful work as *vita activa* is also a means of maintaining good health.

For our context, we would like to present volunteer from the perspective of research on the *meaning of life* (Schnell, 2020). According to this, meaningful work is characterized by four peculiarities: significance, purpose, coherence, and belonging. Schnell and Hoffmann (2020, p. 2) provide the following explanations:

- *Significance* means the "perceived impact of personal action, or non-action."
- *Purpose* refers to the "availability of a direction, serving as a compass when it comes to making decisions and choosing goals."
- *Coherence* describes a "sense of comprehensibility and consistency."
- *Belonging* means "perceiving oneself as part of something larger than the self, as having a place in this world."

With reference to volunteer work, we would like to make two additions. Firstly, volunteer work—as meaningful work—is "*temporally complex*" (Bailey & Madden, 2017): with its own temporal work rhythm, allowing for personal control of time, for working slowly but diligently, etc. The main resource we invest in volunteer work is our time, and this, unlike money or reputation, is in principle non-renewable.

Secondly, volunteer work is *deeply social*. Bailey et al. (2019) call this a paradox of meaningful work: One must be with others to get to oneself: "meaningfulness arises in the context of self-fulfillment and self-actualization, yet it is dependent on the 'other' for its realization." (p. 490). The deeply social character of volunteer work can be very aptly represented by how Karl E. Weick (1995) described sensemaking in organizations: It is grounded in a person's *identity construction*; it is driven by *plausibility* rather than accuracy; it is *ongoing* (now, retroactively, in constant adaptation); and it is *enactive*: With volunteer work, the world is set up as it should be ("enacted"), even if it is still far from any notion of perfection.

Volunteer work means the donation of meaning by personal activity, and—according to Arendt—a "disclosure of the agent in speech and action" (Arendt, 1958, chap. 24). We close with three quotations, which prove representatively, for

---

[1] The work of Theo Wehner's Zurich research group (and Wehner & Güntert, 2015) was based on the activity theory of Leont'ev (Leontjew, 1981, 1982; cf. Wehner et al., 2015), which, however, is not available in English.

many, how much volunteer work turns around the motive of meaningful work and enactive sensemaking:

- "I can make myself useful anywhere. But here I get something back that I usually don't get so easily. What it really is, I can't say so easily—and I don't have to" (43-year-old coordinator of a hospice group).
- "To experience meaning is what I am all about! If I were paid for the work, I would no longer do it, then I would have to make comparisons, deal with performance and who knows what else" (64-year-old volunteer at a university hospital).
- "[. . .] if the whole thing doesn't make sense to me anymore, then I can and would stop immediately; I don't need to know what makes sense to someone else—I have a feeling for it" (58-year-old volunteer with the Swiss Red Cross).

Meaningful Work: A Study on Firefighters A key difference between volunteer work and gainful employment is that volunteer work is usually unpaid, while pay and the accompanying livelihood security is a feature and important motive for gainful employment. Compensation seems to have a strong influence on motives, as empirical findings show that motive structures differ among volunteers once the commitment is remunerated (Strubel et al., 2016). In this context, Lehmann et al. (2018) investigated and compared the *experience of meaning in life* in gainful employment and volunteer work using the example of firefighters. The central question was whether there are differences in the experiences of meaning when the activities in gainful employment and volunteer work are the same or at least similar in many aspects.

For the study, 45 professional and 100 volunteer firefighters from Germany were surveyed. To investigate meaning in life, the study participants answered the *Sources of Meaning and Meaning in Life Questionnaire* (*Fragebogen zu Lebensbedeutungen und Lebenssinn*: Schnell & Becker, 2007) that distinguishes 26 sources of meanings. The results of the study are clear (see Fig. 1.2): Although professional and volunteer firefighters operate in a similar activity environment and even have more similarities than differences in their motivational structures and job satisfaction (Kals et al., 2016), the results clearly show differences in the expressions of some sources of meanings. *That is, volunteer firefighters are more likely to draw on more diverse sources of meanings than professional firefighters.*

Particularly noteworthy is the source of meaning "*generativity.*" Generativity as a central developmental task describes the feeling of leaving a trace in life; a reverberation that lasts beyond one's own death. Generativity also characterizes the ability to take responsibility and care for subsequent generations. If the individual does not succeed in mastering the developmental task of generativity, he or she falls into a health-threatening stagnation (Erikson, 1982), which is often described and perceived as a midlife crisis.

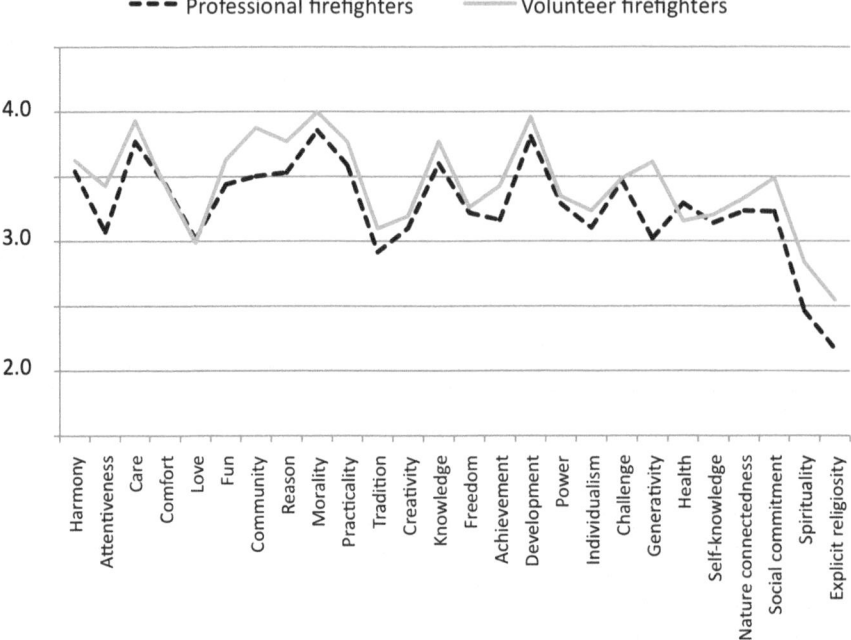

Fig. 1.2 Experience of meaning in life among professional vs. volunteering firefighters (data from Lehmann et al., 2018). Values range between one (least) and five (most)

1.4 The Voluntary Engagement of Older People

For various reasons, high expectations are associated with the voluntary commitment of older people. From a sociopolitical perspective, the volunteer work of this population group can be understood *as a valuable resource*, as older people have freer access to their time and can contribute a wealth of experience. Furthermore, volunteering is seen *as an opportunity for older people*, as it offers opportunities to participate in social life, to experience social inclusion as well as recognition, and to be able to engage in meaningful activity. It is therefore not surprising that in Austria, too, the highest participation rate of 57% occurred within the 60–69 age group, and that 43% of 70–79 year olds still volunteer (BMASK, 2016, p. 17).

Furthermore, the engagement of older people benefits not only volunteer organizations and society as a whole but also the individuals themselves. A large number of studies have shown that volunteering by older people is associated with better physical and mental health (Li & Ferraro, 2005; Luoh & Herzog, 2002), lower probability of illness, better mental well-being, greater life satisfaction (Onyx & Warburton, 2003), lower mortality (Harris & Thoresen, 2005), and better general well-being (Baker et al., 2005). This list includes aspects that people want for old age or need for successful aging (Rowe & Kahn, 1997).

A meta-analysis (Okun & Schultz, 2003), which included all available and comparable studies, showed that in old age certain functions are indeed mentioned more often or less often than by younger volunteers. Above all, the career function, but also the experience function, i.e., the desire to learn new things, becomes less important with increasing age. In turn, the importance of the *social adaptation function* increases. This means that people become more active voluntarily with increasing age because their circles of acquaintances and friends are also active voluntarily. This can be explained by the socioemotional selectivity theory (Carstensen et al., 1999), which states that as people age, they become increasingly aware that their lifespan is limited. As a result, older people begin to focus more on the present and not just the future, which results in a shift in primary goals in life. Close social acquaintances become more important, while the pursuit of success and the acquisition of new knowledge and experiences become less important (Fung et al., 2001).

References

Arendt, H. (1958). *The human condition*. The University of Chicago Press.
Bailey, C., Lips-Wiersma, M., Madden, A., Yeoman, R., Thompson, M., & Chalofsky, N. (2019). The five paradoxes of meaningful work: Introduction to the special issue 'meaningful work: Prospects for the 21st century'. *Journal of Management Studies, 56*(3), 481–499.
Bailey, C., & Madden, A. (2017). Time reclaimed: Temporality and the experience of meaningful work. *Work, Employment and Society, 31*(1), 3–18.
Baker, L., Cahalin, L. P., Gerst, K., & Burr, J. A. (2005). Productive activities and subjective well-being among older adults: The influence of number of activities and time commitment. *Social Indicators Research, 73*, 431–458.
BMASK Bundesministerium für Arbeit, Soziales und Konsumentenschutz. (2016). *Freiwilligenengagement Bevölkerungsbefragung 2016, Studienbericht*. BMASK.
BMFSFJ Bundesministerium für Familie, Senioren, Frauen und Jugend. (2021). *Freiwilliges Engagement in Deutschland. Zentrale Ergebnisse des Fünften Deutschen-Freiwilligensurveys (FWS 2019)*. BMFSFJ. www.bmfsfj.de
Carstensen, L., Isaacowitz, D. M., & Charles, S. T. (1999). Taking time seriously: A theory of socioemotional selectivity. *American Psychologist, 54*, 165–181.
Erikson, E. H. (1982). *Childhood and society*. Norton.
Eurofound. (2017). *Third European quality of life survey - Quality of life in Europe: Impacts of the crisis*. Publications Office of the European Union.
Freitag, M., Manatschal, A., Ackermann, K., & Ackermann, M. (Eds.). (2016). *Freiwilligen-Monitor Schweiz 2016*. Seismo.
Fung, H. H., Carstensen, L. L., & Lang, F. R. (2001). Age-related patterns in social networks among European Americans and African Americans: Implications for socioemotional selectivity across the life span. *International Journal of Aging and Human Development, 52*, 185–206.
Harris, A., & Thoresen, C. (2005). Volunteering is associated with delayed mortality in older people: Analysis of the longitudinal study of aging. *Journal of Health Psychology, 10*, 739–752.
Kals, E., Strubel, I., Vaganian, L., Güntert, S., & Wehner, T. (2016). Freiwilligenarbeit und Erwerbsarbeit am Beispiel der Feuerwehr: mehr Gemeinsamkeiten als Unterschiede. *Wirtschaftspsychologie, 2*, 67–79.
Lamprecht, M., Fischer, A., & Stamm, H. (Eds.). (2020). *Freiwilligen-Monitor Schweiz 2020*. Seismo.

Lehmann, A., Wehner, T., & Ramos, R. (2018). *Freiwilligenarbeit – psycho-soziale Ressource und sinngenerierende Tätigkeit. Fehlzeiten-Report 2018* (pp. 235–243). Springer.
Leontjew, A. N. (1981). Psychologie des Abbilds. *Forum Kritische Psychologie, 9*, 5–19.
Leontjew, A. N. (1982). *Tätigkeit, Bewusstsein, Persönlichkeit* (2nd ed.). Volk und Wissen.
Li, Y.-G., & Ferraro, K. F. (2005). Volunteering and depression in later life: Social benefit or selection processes? *Journal of Health and Social Behavior, 46*, 68–84.
Luoh, M.-C., & Herzog, R. A. (2002). Individual consequences of volunteer and paid work in old age: Health and mortality. *Journal of Health and Social Behavior, 43*, 490–509.
Mieg, H. A. (2001). *The social psychology of expertise: Case studies in research, professional domains, and expert roles*. Lawrence Erlbaum.
Mieg, H. A., & Wehner, T. (2002). *Frei-gemeinnützige Arbeit: Eine Analyse aus Sicht der Arbeits- und Organisationspsychologie*. Technische Universität Hamburg-Harburg, Arbeitswissenschaft. Online available.
Okun, M. A., & Schultz, A. (2003). Age and motives for volunteering: Testing hypotheses derived from socioemotional selectivity theory. *Psychology & Aging, 18*, 231–239.
Onyx, J., & Warburton, J. (2003). Volunteering and health among older people: A review. *Australasian Journal on Aging, 22*, 65–69.
Rosenkranz, D., & Görtler, E. (2002). Woher kommen in Zukunft die Freiwilligen? Demographische Überlegungen zum Sozialen Management. In D. Rosenkranz & A. Weber (Eds.), *Freiwilligenarbeit. Einführung in das Management von Ehrenamtlichen in der Sozialen Arbeit*. Juventa.
Rowe, J. W., & Kahn, R. L. (1997). Successful aging. *The Gerontologist, 37*, 433–440.
Schnell, T. (2020). *The psychology of meaning in life*. Routledge.
Schnell, T., & Becker, P. (2007). *Fragebogen zu Lebensbedeutungen und Lebenssinn: LEBE*. Hogrefe.
Schnell, T., & Hoffmann, C. (2020). ME-work: Development and validation of a modular meaning in work inventory. *Frontiers in Psychology, 11*, 3405.
Simonson, J., Vogel, C., & Tesch-Römer, C. (Eds.). (2017). *Freiwilliges Engagement in Deutschland: Der Deutsche Freiwilligensurvey 2014*. Springer VS.
Stadelmann, I., Traunmüller, R., Gundelach, B., & Freitag, M. (2010). *Freiwilligen-Monitor Schweiz 2010*. Seismo.
Strubel, I. T., Krämer, K., & Kals, E. (2016). Bezahlt und dennoch freiwillig tätig? Ein Motivvergleich entlohnter und nicht entlohnter Freiwilligenarbeit. *Zürcher Buchbeiträge zur Psychologie der Arbeit, 4*, 155–166.
Wehner, T., & Güntert, S. T. (Eds.). (2015). *Psychologie der Freiwilligenarbeit*. Springer.
Wehner, T., Güntert, S. T., Neufeind, M., & Mieg, H. A. (2015). Frei-gemeinnützige Tätigkeit: Freiwilligenarbeit als Forschungs- und Gestaltungsfeld der Arbeits- und Organisationspsychologie. In T. Wehner & S. T. Güntert (Eds.), *Psychologie der Freiwilligenarbeit* (pp. 3–22). Springer.
Weick, K. E. (1995). *Sensemaking in organizations*. Sage.

Open Access This chapter is licensed under the terms of the Creative Commons Attribution 4.0 International License (http://creativecommons.org/licenses/by/4.0/), which permits use, sharing, adaptation, distribution and reproduction in any medium or format, as long as you give appropriate credit to the original author(s) and the source, provide a link to the Creative Commons license and indicate if changes were made.

The images or other third party material in this chapter are included in the chapter's Creative Commons license, unless indicated otherwise in a credit line to the material. If material is not included in the chapter's Creative Commons license and your intended use is not permitted by statutory regulation or exceeds the permitted use, you will need to obtain permission directly from the copyright holder.

Chapter 2
Volunteer Work as a Matter of Motivation

Hardly any other topic has stimulated more research on volunteering than the question of what motivates volunteers and keeps them committed to their engagement. This chapter first presents an established approach to classifying and measuring the diverse motives for volunteering. Subsequently, this approach is extended and reflected on from the perspective of self-determination theory.

2.1 The Functional Approach

Clary et al. (1998) applied the so-called functional approach to the analysis of volunteer work. Inspired by research on the functions that are served by attitudes, they shed light on the multi-faceted motivational foundations of volunteer work. What psychological functions can volunteer work fulfill? Their findings describe the following six motivational functions:

- *Values:* Volunteers can express their own values through voluntary work; those values typically related to solidarity and humanitarian concerns (example statement: "I can do something for a cause that is important to me").
- *Understanding:* Volunteer work provides the opportunity to gain experience, acquire new skills, and become a competent actor in a certain domain; understanding oneself better also falls into this category (example: "I can explore my strengths").
- *Career:* The professional career can be promoted by volunteer work, be it through networking or the usefulness of volunteering as an attractive asset listed in one's CV (example: "Volunteering will help me to succeed in my chosen profession").
- *Social:* Performing volunteer work might reflect the expectations of important others; through their involvement, volunteers might signal their integration into

that group of family and friends (example: "People I am close to want me to volunteer").
- *Enhancement:* Volunteer work can increase one's self-esteem; as a volunteer, you feel needed (example: "My volunteering makes me feel better about myself").
- *Protective:* Volunteer work may protect from negatively experienced feelings and can offer distraction from worries (example: "No matter how bad I have been feeling, volunteering helps me to forget about it").

To record these functions of volunteer work, Clary et al. (1998) developed a corresponding measurement instrument in the form of a questionnaire: the *Volunteer Functions Inventory*. With five statements per function, volunteers rate the importance of this aspect in motivating their own voluntary work. The Volunteer Functions Inventory is not only suitable for comparative research (between countries or different types of volunteer work), but can also be used in practice, for example, to gain an overview of the motives of volunteers within an organization. Studies that have used the Volunteer Functions Inventory report that the *values* and *understanding* function accurately represents respondents' motivations for volunteering (e.g., Oostlander et al., 2014a).

Key to the functional approach to volunteerism is the assumption that different people can perform the same volunteer work and still hold fundamentally diverse motivations for the respective activity. One person may volunteer to visit hospital patients in order to support lonely people and thus express personal values. For another person, this commitment may be linked primarily to an ambition to work at that hospital in the future. Furthermore, volunteer work can fulfill several independent psychological functions simultaneously for the same person. Expressing humanitarian concerns while also being interested in acquiring skills and gaining a new perspective on things is certainly no contradiction at all.

The functionalist perspective on volunteer work offers ideas on how to keep volunteers committed to their activity. The benefits associated with volunteer work should match the respective motivational functions expressed by the volunteers (Stukas et al., 2009). Volunteer managers, for example, who acknowledge the volunteers' tasks and efforts in a document that can be added to a résumé, provide a clear match for the career function.

2.2 Extensions of the Functional Approach

The value function, as measured by the Volunteer Functions Inventory, is clearly aligned with the values of solidarity and compassion for people in need. Numerous organizations in which volunteers are active pursue the goal of changing the root causes (e.g., political and social conditions) of suffering and need. Fighting for social justice can be a strong motive for volunteering in human rights organizations, for example. For this reason, Jiranek et al. (2015) propose the *social justice function* as an extension of the functional approach. It can be empirically demonstrated that this motivational function, in addition to the already established functions of the Volunteer Functions Inventory, explains volunteers' intention to continue their engagement (Jiranek et al., 2013).

A second example of how to extend the functional approach comes from a significantly different area of volunteer work. Some volunteering activities offer immediate and attractive opportunities to experience something extraordinary that is not possible in other areas of life. People who volunteer for a major international event such as the Olympic Games or soccer championships, for example, experience this unique or rare event first-hand, take part in the action and get an exclusive look behind the scenes of the event. In other words, the activity itself has a high reward value for people who are interested in the subject area in question. Güntert et al. (2015) describe this motive for volunteering as an *experiential function* and show that for volunteers for whom this experiential function is very important, tasks providing autonomy in decision-making are particularly important and satisfying.

These are only two examples of extensions to the functional approach. Adding or refining some of the original six functions suggested by Clary et al. (1998) does not challenge the basic tenets of that framework. Rather, such extensions illustrate that volunteer work may serve a remarkably wide range of functions. This multiplicity of functions can be addressed by volunteer managers to fine-tune the volunteer task and "tailor" benefits to attract and retain a diverse group of volunteers.

2.3 A Self-Determination Theory Perspective on Volunteer Motives

For each person, volunteering may serve multiple functions simultaneously. This key functionalist notion, however, does not imply that all volunteer motives show similarly strong associations with important outcomes. A study by Stukas et al. (2016) demonstrated that self-oriented motives and other-oriented motives were differentially associated with volunteers' satisfaction and sustained volunteering. Most importantly, the *value function*—the motive to volunteer in order to express one's values of solidarity and humanity—correlates more strongly with the satisfaction, the intention to continue the commitment, and also the health of the volunteers than functions that focus on increasing self-esteem or direct personal benefit. To shed light on these correlational patterns, self-determination theory can be used as a framework to interpret the quality of motivation that is inherent in various types of volunteer functions. Some types of motivation go hand in hand with the experience of freedom, volition, and self-determination, while other motives are associated with the experience of being controlled, under pressure, and alien to one's true self.

The core idea of *self-determination theory* (Deci & Ryan, 2000; Gagné & Deci, 2005; Güntert, 2015) is to take a *qualitative* perspective on motivation beyond a simple quantitative one. Different people can show similarly strong effort when performing a task, but still experience disparate emotions. One volunteer confronted

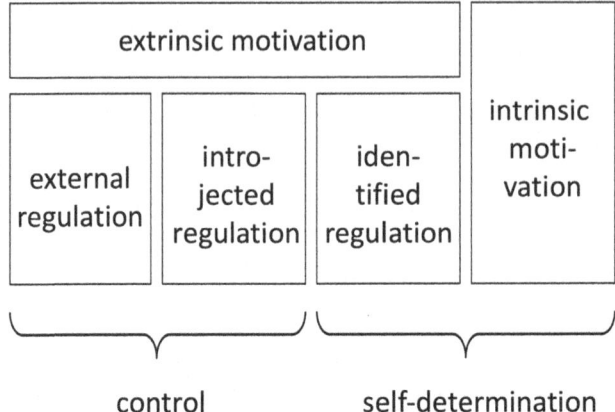

Fig. 2.1 Four types of motivation according to self-determination theory

with a challenge might experience freedom, choice, and flow while solving this problem. Another person might show similar diligence and effort, but may lack the experience of joy and volition completely and instead be driven by pressure from outside or by the fear that their self-worth is at stake.

Self-determination theory differentiates between self-determined and controlled types of motivation. Figure 2.1 links the different types of motivation to the experience of either self-determination or control. The quality of these types of motivation is described using examples from the context of volunteering:

- *Intrinsic motivation* represents the prototype of self-determined motivation. Performing the activity is rewarding in itself. Intrinsic motivation refers to the search for optimal challenge and personal growth. Volunteers who are interested in and want to learn more about a specific topic show intrinsic motivation. They are absorbed in the activity and may experience flow (cf. Csikszentmihályi, 1990). No rewards or punishments are needed; the simple joy in the activity is sufficient to sustain the effort. Some fundamental aspects of volunteer work increase the likelihood that intrinsic motivation is experienced. Volunteers choose organizations and tasks based on their interest and talent. If they were to experience excessive demands, volunteers can probably adjust their involvement more easily than paid employees who make their living out of a similar type of work.
- *Identified regulation* of extrinsic motivation is a second type of self-determined motivation characterized by the experience of freedom and choice. Labeling intrinsic motivation as the prototype of self-determination does not imply that extrinsic motivation is, by default, associated with pressure, control, and alienation. Behavior that is extrinsically motivated is instrumental to some goal that is clearly separated from the activity itself. Extrinsically motivated activities are often not, per se, interesting or fun. An example from the volunteer context illustrates the conceptual difference. Volunteers supporting an animal shelter

2.3 A Self-Determination Theory Perspective on Volunteer Motives

Table 2.1 Correlations between types of motivation and indicators of successful volunteering

Sample and target size	Intrinsic motivation	Identified regulation	Introjected regulation	External regulation
Healthcare sector (124 participants; Millette & Gagné, 2008)				
Satisfaction	0.33**	0.23**	0.03	−0.22*
Intention to leave the organization	−0.17†	−0.20*	−0.18*	0.17†
Performance	0.07	0.09	−0.02	−0.03
Social services and education (349 participants; Haivas et al., 2012)				
Satisfaction	0.50**	0.29**	0.14**	0.07**
Intention to leave the organization	−0.18**	−0.16**	−0.16*	0.02
Work engagement	0.31**	0.37**	0.11**	−0.27**
Health and social services (1845 participants; Oostlander et al., 2014b)				
Intention to continue the activity	0.19**	0.12**	0.05*	0.03
Work engagement	0.58**	0.45**	0.34**	0.24**

Non-negative values (range 0 to 1) represent positive correlation strength. Negative values represent inverse correlation (maximum −1). The table was slightly adjusted and taken from Güntert, 2015. Significance levels: † $p < 0.10$. * $p < 0.05$. ** $p < 0.01$

might take on the task of walking dogs on a regular basis; for many people, this volunteer task will be rewarding in itself as they enjoy the company of a dog. The same volunteers might also help clean the cages at the animal shelter; for most people, this strenuous and dirty work will not be experienced as fun and interesting, but rather as important and useful for a goal beyond the activity itself, that is, to keep the animals healthy and attractive for adoption. If a person fully understands the importance of a task and identifies with the respective values, the regulation of that behavior is endorsed by one's core sense of self.

- *Introjected regulation* of extrinsic motivation represents a controlled type of motivation. The activity is not fully supported by the person's core sense of self, but rather regulated by feelings of guilt, shame, or the need to please other people. Volunteers who continue their engagement not because of strong identification with the goals and values, but rather because they do not want to miss the attention or cannot distance themselves from expectations, experience this quality of motivation.
- *External regulation* of extrinsic motivation represents the most controlled type of motivation. The behavior is regulated by rewards or punishments that are external to the activity and often under the control of other people. In the context of volunteering, this quality of motivation may be observed when volunteers mainly focus on tangible benefits such as boosting their career using a prestigious voluntary role.

The four types of motivation described by self-determination theory are differentially related to volunteer outcomes. Table 2.1 shows, for three different samples,

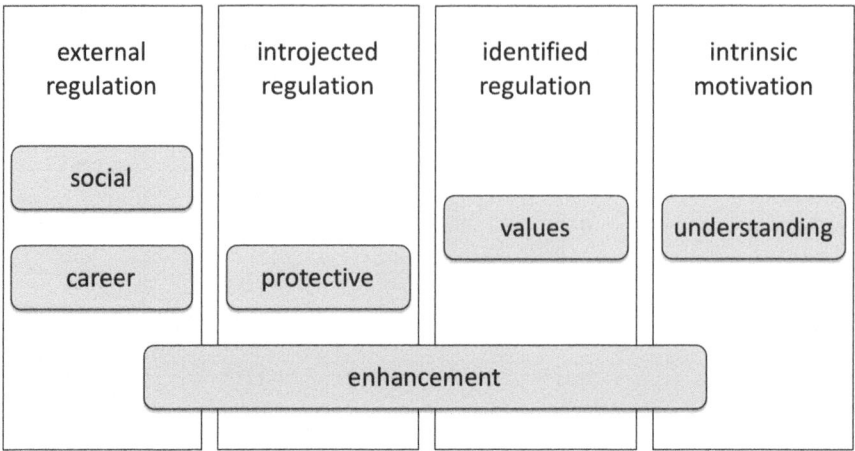

Fig. 2.2 Linking four types of motivation according to self-determination theory to six motives according to the functional approach

the correlations between the four qualities of motivation and various indicators of successful volunteering.

Overall, *self-determined types of motivation*—that is, intrinsic motivation and identified regulation of extrinsic motivation—are more strongly related than are controlled types of motivation to favorable outcomes. In a longitudinal study by Güntert and Wehner (2015), self-determined motivation was positively associated with both general and organization-specific role identities of volunteers several months later. This finding is in line with self-determination theory's assumption that *the self-determined quality of motivation is both an expression and a prerequisite of personal growth and an integrated sense of self*.

Using the framework of self-determination theory, the findings of Stukas et al. (2016) can be revisited. Volunteers' motives, as described by the functional approach were *differentially related to favorable volunteer outcomes*. As illustrated in Fig. 2.2, the four qualities of self-determined vs. controlled motivation presented in Fig. 2.1 can be systematically linked to the six motivational functions—i.e., volunteers' motives—described by Clary et al. (1998):

- Values: The motive to express one's values through volunteering is clearly aligned with *identified regulation's* focus on endorsing values.
- Understanding: The learning opportunities as a motive for volunteering are linked to the element of curiosity inherent in *intrinsic motivation*.
- Career: Boosting one's career through volunteering puts emphasis on the usefulness of that activity; the external evaluation of one's performance as a volunteer might trigger the experience of *external regulation and control*.
- Social: The concern about other people's expectations as a motive for volunteering clearly links to *controlled types of motivation*.

- Enhancement: This volunteer function can be associated with *both controlled and self-determined types of motivation*. Self-worth contingencies (e.g., being proud) can be linked to introjected regulation; however, enjoying the company of others (e.g., making friends) is associated with intrinsic motivation.
- Protective: This motive is associated with the usefulness of volunteering to address negative emotions; similarly to the enhancement function, this motive is linked to self-worth contingencies and, thus, to *controlled types of motivation*.

Taken together, the concept of self-determination not only describes a relevant aspect of the volunteer experience, but also explains the differential impact of various motives as described by the functional approach (see also Güntert et al., 2016).

References

Clary, E. G., Snyder, M., Ridge, R. D., Copeland, J., Stukas, A. A., Haugen, J., & Miene, P. (1998). Understanding and assessing the motivations of volunteers. *Journal of Personality and Social Psychology, 74*, 1516–1530.

Csikszentmihályi, M. (1990). *Flow: The psychology of optimal experience*. Harper & Row.

Deci, E. L., & Ryan, R. M. (2000). The "what" and "why" of goal pursuits: Human needs and the self-determination of behavior. *Psychological Inquiry, 11*, 227–268.

Gagné, M., & Deci, E. L. (2005). Self-determination theory and work motivation. *Journal of Organizational Behavior, 26*, 331–362.

Güntert, S. T. (2015). Selbstbestimmung in der Freiwilligenarbeit. In T. Wehner & S. T. Güntert (Eds.), *Psychologie der Freiwilligenarbeit* (pp. 77–93). Springer.

Güntert, S. T., Neufeind, M., & Wehner, T. (2015). Motives for event volunteering: Extending the functional approach. *Nonprofit and Voluntary Sector Quarterly, 44*(4), 686–707.

Güntert, S. T., Strubel, I. T., Kals, E., & Wehner, T. (2016). The quality of volunteers' motives: Integrating the functional approach and self-determination theory. *The Journal of Social Psychology, 156*, 310–327.

Güntert, S. T., & Wehner, T. (2015). The impact of self-determined motivation on volunteer role identities. *Personality and Individual Differences, 78*, 14–18.

Haivas, S., Hofmans, J., & Pepermans, R. (2012). Self-determination theory as a framework for exploring the impact of the organizational context on volunteer motivation. *Nonprofit and Voluntary Sector Quarterly, 41*, 1195–1214.

Jiranek, P., Kals, E., Humm, J. S., Strubel, I. T., & Wehner, T. (2013). Volunteering as a means to an equal end? The impact of a social justice function on intention to volunteer. *The Journal of Social Psychology, 153*, 520–541.

Jiranek, P., Wehner, T., & Kals, E. (2015). Soziale Gerechtigkeit – ein eigenständiges Motiv für Freiwilligenarbeit. In T. Wehner & S. T. Güntert (Eds.), *Psychologie der Freiwilligenarbeit* (pp. 95–108). Springer.

Millette, V., & Gagné, M. (2008). Designing volunteers' tasks to maximize motivation, satisfaction and performance. *Motivation and Emotion, 32*, 11–22.

Oostlander, J., Güntert, S. T., van Schie, S., & Wehner, T. (2014a). Leadership and volunteer motivation: A study using self-determination theory. *Nonprofit and Voluntary Sector Quarterly, 43,* 869–889.

Oostlander, J., Güntert, S. T., van Schie, S., & Wehner, T. (2014b). Volunteer functions inventory (VFI). Psychometric properties and construct validity of the German adaptation. *Diagnostica, 60,* 73–85.

Stukas, A. A., Hoye, R., Nicholson, M., Brown, K. M., & Aisbett, L. (2016). Motivations to volunteer and their associations with volunteers' Well-being. *Nonprofit and Voluntary Sector Quarterly, 45,* 112–132.

Stukas, A. A., Worth, K. A., Clary, E. G., & Snyder, M. (2009). The matching of motivations to affordances in the volunteer environment. *Nonprofit and Voluntary Sector Quarterly, 38,* 5–28.

Open Access This chapter is licensed under the terms of the Creative Commons Attribution 4.0 International License (http://creativecommons.org/licenses/by/4.0/), which permits use, sharing, adaptation, distribution and reproduction in any medium or format, as long as you give appropriate credit to the original author(s) and the source, provide a link to the Creative Commons license and indicate if changes were made.

The images or other third party material in this chapter are included in the chapter's Creative Commons license, unless indicated otherwise in a credit line to the material. If material is not included in the chapter's Creative Commons license and your intended use is not permitted by statutory regulation or exceeds the permitted use, you will need to obtain permission directly from the copyright holder.

Chapter 3
Volunteer Work as an Organizational Task

3.1 Volunteering as a Process

The initial decision to volunteer should be distinguished from the willingness to continue to do so and to show effort. In the process of volunteering, new factors influencing motivation become apparent. The specific nature of the tasks that volunteers undertake, the behavior of the volunteer coordinator, contact with the people who are to benefit from the commitment, cooperation with other volunteers and professional staff of the organization, the reactions of the private environment, and the policies and strategies of the organization as a whole: these factors and many more influence whether volunteers develop a feeling of solidarity during the course of their engagement, and a commitment to the organization (e.g., Alfes et al., 2017; Grant, 2012; McBey et al., 2017; Nencini et al., 2016). To further emphasize the process perspective on volunteering, Chacón et al. (2007) developed a *three-stage model of volunteers' duration* (see Fig. 3.1).

For volunteers who work in an organization over an extended period, the role they play becomes an essential part of their own identity (Penner, 2002; Piliavin & Callero, 1991; Piliavin et al., 2002; Thoits, 2021). Grube and Piliavin (2000) distinguish between a general role identity as a volunteer and an *organization-specific role identity*. If this stage is reached in the process of volunteering, the commitment is less easily called into question, even in the face of adversity and disappointment, because volunteering expresses an important aspect of one's own personality. In its strongest form, role identity means that the person engaging in this activity can be the person you truly are or want to be—in addition to other roles, of course. For organizations that want to work with volunteers, it is important to encourage the development of an organization-specific role identity, because volunteers who have developed a general role identity and who have a specific good cause at heart may decide to divert their limited voluntary time to other (competing) organizations within the field.

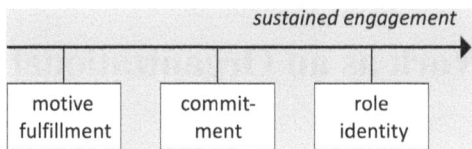

Fig. 3.1 Functional approach and role identity theory in a temporal context (cf. Chacón et al., 2007); figure taken from van Schie et al. (2015). Chacón et al. (2007) developed this three-stage approach based on the functional approach (Clary et al., 1998; Stukas et al., 2009) and the role identity approach (Grube & Piliavin, 2000). This process perspective was empirically corroborated by Vecina et al. (2010)

3.2 Three Basic Psychological Needs as Orientation

Self-determination theory offers an explanation of why some particular motives for volunteering are more closely associated with desirable goals. However, when it comes to designing volunteer work in a way that is self-fulfilling for the volunteers themselves and useful for the people and organizations that benefit from it, self-determination theory offers further concepts that provide orientation for such design considerations.

Basic psychological needs can be distilled from studies on self-determined or controlled types of motivation. The satisfaction of these basic needs is considered necessary for people to succeed in a fulfilling life—characterized by self-determination and freedom. Three basic psychological needs are identified (see Deci & Ryan, 2000):

- *Need for competence*: People strive to deal competently with their social and material environment; expanding their own skills and abilities is a basic human need.
- *Need for autonomy*: people strive to experience themselves as the origin of their own actions; having choices and not being subjected to any constraints is considered a basic need.
- *Need for relatedness*: For healthy psychological development, people depend on being able to feel involved in close and often cultivated relationships with other people.

These three basic needs can be either *satisfied or frustrated* in different life contexts. Whether self-determined motivation can be experienced depends on the satisfaction of these needs, as illustrated by the following example: A volunteer is introduced very well to their area of responsibility and has the opportunity to receive continuous training in order to take on new tasks during the course of their commitment (need for competence). The coordinator encourages the volunteer to make their own decisions, responds with honest interest to questions, even if they contain criticism, and does not closely monitor the volunteer (need for autonomy). Finally, the volunteer feels part of a team; the atmosphere is characterized by mutual respect; there are other people involved in the volunteer work with whom they can also talk openly about personal issues; and socializing also finds its place (need for relatedness).

According to self-determination theory, the conditions are thus created, firstly for intrinsic motivation (the experience of optimal challenge and the experience of being absorbed in the activity), secondly for identified regulation (the insight into the necessity and meaning of various tasks, even if they are uninteresting or even unpleasant). While one might expect cultural differences in the relative importance of each need (for example, the need for autonomy might be higher in individualist than in collectivist societies), interestingly, *each* basic need is equally essential for psychological well-being throughout a broad range of highly varied cultures (Deci & Ryan, 2008).

3.3 Neglected Importance of Tasks and Organization

When designing volunteer work, it is possible to draw on the rich experience of work and organizational psychology in the context of gainful employment (for an overview of various concepts, see van Schie et al., 2015). Although theories should not be blindly transferred, but should always include the basic characteristics of volunteer work, it is nevertheless worthwhile for practitioners to be aware of established starting points, for example, in the design of tasks.

A classic concept for the evaluation and design of tasks, which is still used for orientation after 40 years, is Hackman and Oldham's (1976) Job Characteristics Model. This model identifies five job characteristics that make up the motivational potential of a work activity (the following sample statements are formulated in relation to a volunteer activity):

- *Skill variety*: ("In my volunteer activity I do many different things").
- *Task identity*: ("My volunteer activity is structured in such a way that I carry out a complete work process from start to finish").
- *Task significance*: ("My volunteer activity has a significant impact on the lives of other people").
- *Autonomy*: ("With my volunteer activity I can make many decisions independently").
- *Feedback*: from the activity itself ("When performing my volunteer activity I can easily determine how well I am working").

Volunteering with high motivation potential strengthens both intrinsic motivation and the identified regulation of those tasks that are primarily useful and necessary but not necessarily interesting. Several studies (e.g., Maas et al., 2021; Millette & Gagné, 2008; Neufeind et al., 2013; van Schie et al., 2014, 2015) show that task design also pays off in the area of volunteering in order to support sustained engagement.

Making volunteer work more motivational does not mean that all tasks need to become cognitively more challenging. Even simpler tasks can be combined to form holistic task packages, and scope for independent decision-making can also be provided for less complex tasks. The activity characteristics "significance" and "feedback" pose a particular challenge. In many volunteer activities, the significance of the task for the lives of others seems so obvious that one might assume that one does not have to become active in making already motivational work even more appealing. Nevertheless, it is worthwhile finding creative ways to strengthen the relationship between volunteers and recipients and to make the impact of volunteering more visible. The concept of "relational job design" (Grant, 2007) provides valuable inspiration in this respect.

A striking feature of the organizational context is undoubtedly the *leadership* theme (for an overview, see Zaccaro et al., 2008). Not only in paid employment but also in volunteer work, managers or coordinators can have a positive influence on the motivation, satisfaction, and continuation intentions of their paid employees or unpaid staff (e.g., Benevene et al., 2020; Boezeman & Ellemers, 2014; Cho et al., 2020; Dwyer et al., 2013; Posner, 2015). Although the word leadership is initially surprising in the context of volunteers and unpaid workers, it can also be used to refer to a person who is voluntarily engaged: Formally active volunteers are usually guided by a coordinator from the NPO (non-profit organization). Volunteers themselves also find inadequate leadership and coordination problematic (Mathou, 2010). Some studies have shown that a leadership style that supports autonomy is particularly conducive to the motivation of volunteers (Baard et al., 2004; Haivas et al., 2012; Oostlander et al., 2014). In gainful employment, support for autonomy implies that supervisors show interest in their employees' ideas, express confidence in their abilities, and encourage them to ask questions and be independent. Similarly, coordinators who create a sense of autonomy rather than control can promote motivation and, consequently, positive attitudes and intentions among volunteers.

Another feature of the social environment is the frequent discussion, especially in the context of volunteer work, of *organizational recognition* (Mathou, 2010). For example, Cnaan and Cascio (1998) recommend promoting the intrinsic motivation and productivity of volunteers by means of symbolic rewards (such as thank-you letters, certificates, free training, prizes). Güntert (2007), on the other hand, was able to show that organizational recognition brings not only positive but also negative aspects, as it can also create feelings of "duty" among volunteers. Some volunteers consider their being allowed to work as a volunteer to be recognition enough; additional recognition can therefore cause "slight stress" (see also van Schie et al., 2019). In summary, there is no generic recipe; instead, each setting requires the involvement of volunteers and the authenticity of all.

3.4 The Successful Design of Volunteer Work: An Empirical Study

The empirical study presented in the following was designed on the one hand to test the transferability of concepts from work and organizational psychology to volunteer work (cf. van Schie et al., 2015). On the other hand, it was also intended to identify relevant design characteristics for sustained engagement of volunteers. In this way, we contribute to closing a gap in volunteer research. The reported analyses are based on the information provided by 2222 volunteers from four major social and charitable organizations (NPO) in Switzerland, who were involved in 27 different projects. Over a period of 1.5 years, our study collected design characteristics and then (just over one year after the initial survey) indicators of sustained engagement from the same volunteers; thus, responses from 889 persons are available at two measurement points.

Overall, the results present the following picture:

From the volunteer's point of view, the *characteristics of the tasks* (i.e., varied and significant tasks with direct feedback on work performance) are particularly relevant for an activity that is enjoyable from the volunteer's perspective and that enables liveliness, dedication, and a feeling of being absorbed in the activity itself.

The task characteristics thus also indirectly promote *volunteers' commitment*—to the benefit of the recipients of their assistance—because autonomously motivated volunteers are probably also more committed to the recipients (cf. Weinstein & Ryan, 2010).

The usually high level of satisfaction among volunteers can be maintained or improved if *the components of the organizational framework, such as the flow of information and the coordinators' management style, are consistent*.

The volunteers' loyalty to the NPO, on the other hand, is gained when the volunteers' personal values are aligned with those of the organization. Only the *perceived fit of the values* also promotes the volunteers' willingness to work towards purely organizational concerns (cf. Bahat, 2020).

Who was interviewed?

- *Age*: Half of the volunteers surveyed were aged between 61 and 70, and almost a quarter were between 71 and 80 years old. Only 6.2% were aged 40 or younger.
- *Gender*: Almost two-thirds of the volunteers interviewed were female, although there were large shifts in gender balance depending on the project.
- *Volume of volunteer work*: Four out of five volunteers invest up to five hours per week in their work for the NPO. Only 3.2% commit 11 hours or more per week.
- *Duration of volunteer work*: About 60% of the volunteers have been working for their organization for up to five years, with one in six having been with the organization for 11 years or more.
- *Commitment to recipient and NPO*: Almost half of those surveyed volunteer not just for one but for several organizations at the same time.

The seven largest volunteer projects, which together make up almost 80% of the total sample are:

1. *Integration project*: Volunteers support the integration of foreign-language children and young people through weekly activities at their homes.
2. *Driving service*: Volunteers use their own car to drive people with limited mobility to a doctor's appointment, therapist, etc.
3. *Community work*: Volunteers in communities complement the well-being of older people and strengthen social networks and communities in the locality.
4. *Fiduciary service*: Volunteers support elderly people with commercial and administrative tasks (e.g., tax returns).
5. *Crisis telephone*: Volunteers work in shifts to staff a telephone hotline that is available around the clock to help with worries or problems.
6. *Visiting service*: Volunteers regularly visit and spend time with an older and isolated person.
7. *Sponsorship*: Volunteers act as sponsors for children from needy families, giving them time and attention and possibly helping them with homework.

3.4.1 The Findings for the Task Characteristics

The volunteers in our study rated the work motivation potential of their activities rather positively (see Fig. 3.2). The greatest motivators are the *significance of the activity for other people* and *the holistic nature of the activity* (i.e., involvement in the activity from start to finish). Volunteers, on the other hand, are less likely to

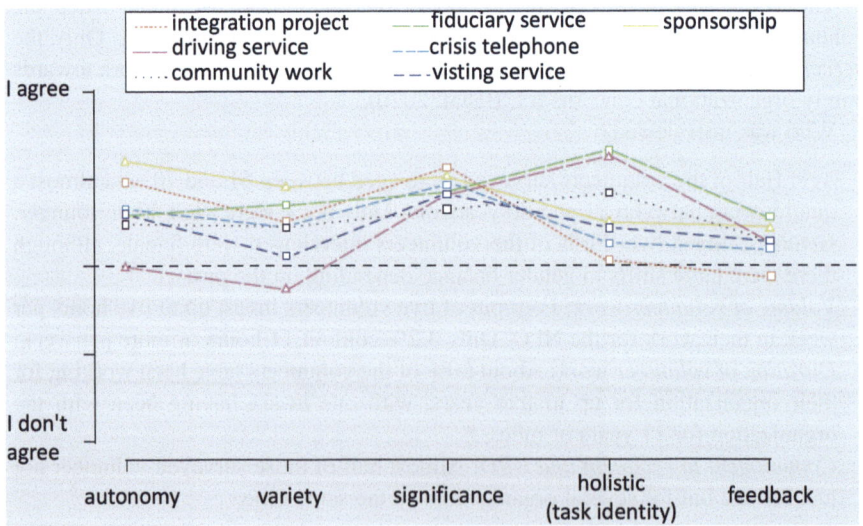

Fig. 3.2 Task characteristics among seven volunteer projects

experience the possibility of decision-making autonomy, the variety of tasks, and direct feedback on their own performance from the tasks themselves. However, even these values are still considered positive.

The projects differ quite considerably in all task characteristics, except for their significance. There are, for instance, variations in the decision-making autonomy, diversity, and holistic nature of the tasks. It is therefore not surprising that the driving service, which is similar to a free taxi service, displays less decision-making autonomy and variety of tasks. On the other hand, the experienced wholeness of the task—for example, an immobile client is collected from home, driven to a doctor's appointment and returned home—is very much present. In contrast, the sponsorship and integration projects show great decision-making autonomy and variety: here, children and young people are cared for in a private environment without the organization being directly involved. Consequently, there is a great deal of freedom to make decisions independently and to arrange the tasks in a varied manner. However, these volunteers experience very little holistic approach to their tasks.

3.4.2 Findings on Organizational Characteristics

Overall, the organizational and social framework is *positively rated by volunteers* (see Fig. 3.3), except when it comes to recognition by NPO employees. It is noticeable that the support provided by the volunteer coordinators is rated as very good, as is the flow of information within the organization and the recognition by the

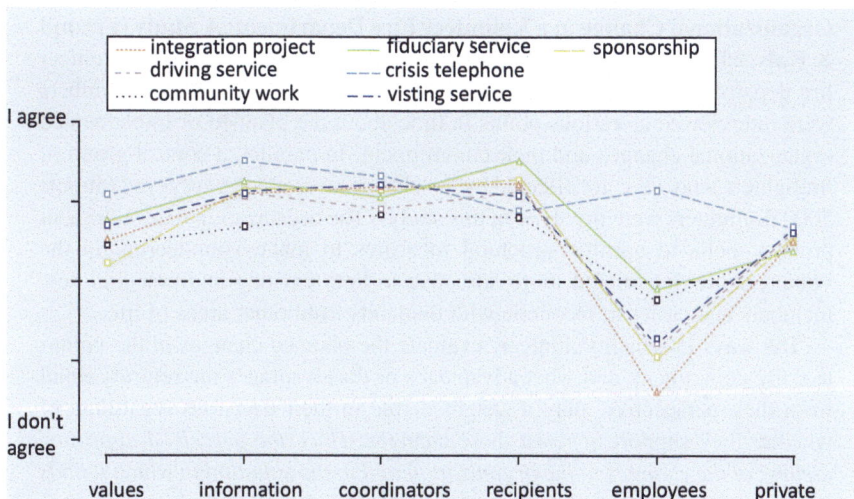

Fig. 3.3 Organizational characteristics (congruence of values; information flow; support by coordinators; recognition by recipients, NPO employees, and one's own private sphere)

recipients. Respondents are less positive concerning the congruence of values and recognition from the private environment.

Projects show the greatest variability in relation to *recognition by NPO employees*. The only project that scores remarkably well here is the crisis telephone, which is probably due to the fact that this institution is almost exclusively run by volunteers and has very few permanent employees. The sponsorship and integration projects, the visiting service, and the transport service, on the other hand, are conducted in private environments or in an environment that is clearly related to the recipients and therefore probably have very little to do with the organization, such that there are likely to be few encounters with employees.

3.4.3 Findings on the Indicators of Sustained Engagement

In general, the interviewed volunteers express extremely high satisfaction, with more than 90% describing themselves as being very satisfied. Less than 1% are little satisfied with their activities. In comparison, the joy of work is also very high but somewhat wider distributed. Almost half of the volunteers describe themselves as having above-average work enthusiasm, while around a quarter have below-average work enthusiasm. The indicators of sustained engagement focus more on NPOs, and the findings must be put in perspective: Only one in seven respondents identified strongly with their organization, two-thirds expressed a medium level of identification, while just over 20% of volunteers regard the NPOs as only a small part of themselves.

> **Organizational Change in a Volunteer Fire Department: A Study (Freund & Kals, 2020)** An organizational development process in a German volunteer fire department was accompanied over several years. The affected members were interviewed at various points in time about the planned or implemented organizational changes and their commitment. In parallel, a control group of firefighters who were not affected by the changes was always surveyed (almost 5000 firefighters were involved in this study). The organizational development process included various structural measures to make volunteering in the volunteer fire department more attractive to both existing and potential new members and easier to reconcile with demands from other areas of life.
>
> The ways in which volunteers evaluate the planned changes in the volunteer fire department, and what advantages or disadvantages the reforms entail from their perspective, play a weighted role in their decisions regardless of whether they support or resist these changes. *Thus, the perceived appropriateness of the changes to the organization and to the situation in which it finds itself emerged in the study as the strongest predictor of commitment to these*

(continued)

3.4 The Successful Design of Volunteer Work: An Empirical Study

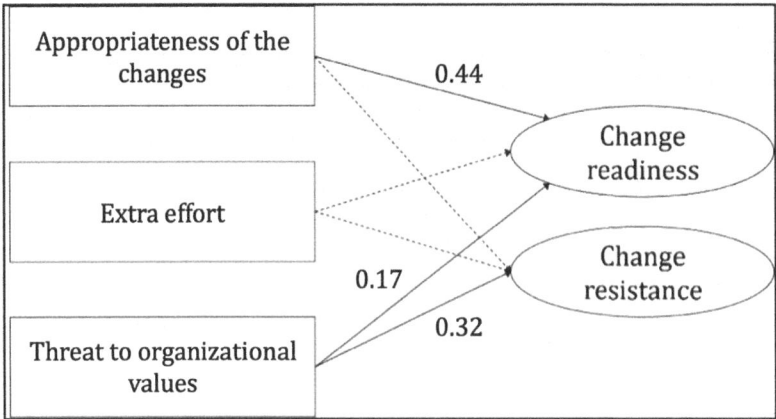

Fig. 3.4. Influence of volunteers' judgments on their willingness to accept or resist proposed changes. The numbers "0.17," "0.32" and "0.44" indicate a strong influence or correlation (beta weights of regression analysis, adapted from Figure 1 in Freund & Kals, 2020)

changes. The extent to which the committed believe planned reforms are meaningful and appropriate for their organization is thus critical in gaining their support (see Fig. 3.4). However, the issue of whether the reforms entail disadvantages for volunteers themselves—in the sense of additional work and effort—does not play a role. This neither prevents volunteers from advocating for change nor motivates them to resist change.

Thus, volunteers invest their time, the main—and often scarce—resource in volunteer work, *without further ado additionally for the further development of the organization*, if they assess its purpose as appropriate and meaningful. Here, the nature of classic volunteer work in particular, in which unpaid time and effort are taken on for the good of the community, clearly comes to bear.

Additional time commitment is not a significant barrier to change in volunteer organizations. However, committed volunteers do resist planned organizational change if they perceive it to *threaten the organization's distinctive values*. A perceived threat to the values important within the fire department emerged as the most significant predictor of resistance to change and as detrimental to support for change. In the case of the volunteer fire department, comradely, traditional-conservative, and hierarchy-related values were relevant in this regard (see also Yarnal et al., 2004). The characteristic values that are important in each case may, of course, vary across organizations due to the heterogeneity of volunteerism.

Furthermore, it is particularly evident in the context of organizational change that consistent individual and organizational values act as a means of binding volunteers to the organization: The more important it is to volunteers

(continued)

that organizational core values remain intact even in the context of change, the more satisfied they are with their volunteer work and the higher their commitment to the organization. This corresponds to the view of volunteering as a value-based and-motivated activity, and once again indicates that value congruence is central to volunteers' commitment to an organization.

References

Alfes, K., Antunes, B., & Shantz, A. D. (2017). The management of volunteers – What can human resources do? A review and research agenda. *The International Journal of Human Resource Management, 28*(1), 62–97.
Baard, P. P., Deci, E. L., & Ryan, R. M. (2004). Intrinsic need satisfaction: A motivational basis of performance and well-being in two work settings. *Journal of Applied Social Psychology, 34*(10), 2045–2068.
Bahat, E. (2020). Person–organization fit and commitment to volunteer organizations. *Voluntas*. Advance online publication. https://doi.org/10.1007/s11266-020-00212-x
Benevene, P., Buonomo, I., & West, M. (2020). The relationship between leadership behaviors and volunteer commitment: The role of volunteer satisfaction. *Frontiers in Psychology, 11*, 602466. https://doi.org/10.3389/fpsyg.2020.602466
Boezeman, E. J., & Ellemers, N. (2014). Volunteer leadership: The role of pride and respect in organizational identification and leadership satisfaction. *Leadership, 10*(2), 160–173.
Chacón, F., Vecina, M. L., & Dàvila, M. C. (2007). The three-stage model of volunteers' duration of service. *Social Behavior and Personality, 35*(5), 627–642.
Cho, H., Wong, Z., & Chiu, W. (2020). The effect of volunteer management on intention to continue volunteering: A mediating role of job satisfaction of volunteers. *SAGE Open, 10*(2), 215824402092058. https://doi.org/10.1177/2158244020920588
Clary, E. G., Snyder, M., Ridge, R. D., Copeland, J., Stukas, A. A., Haugen, J., & Miene, P. (1998). Understanding and assessing the motivations of volunteers. *Journal of Personality and Social Psychology, 74*, 1516–1530.
Cnaan, R. A., & Cascio, T. A. (1998). Performance and commitment. *Journal of Social Service Research, 24*(3–4), 1–37.
Deci, E. L., & Ryan, R. M. (2000). The "what" and "why" of goal pursuits: Human needs and the self-determination of behavior. *Psychological Inquiry, 11*, 227–268.
Deci, E. L., & Ryan, R. M. (2008). Self-determination theory: A macrotheory of human motivation, development, and health. *Canadian Psychology/Psychologie Canadienne, 49*(3), 182–185.
Dwyer, P. C., Bono, J. E., Snyder, M., Nov, O., & Berson, Y. (2013). Sources of volunteer motivation: Transformational leadership and personal motives influence volunteer outcomes. *Nonprofit Management and Leadership, 24*, 181–205.
Freund, S., & Kals, E. (2020). Transformationen in wertebasierten Organisationen. Balance zwischen Bewahren und Verändern. *Konfliktdynamik, 9*(1), 38–46. https://doi.org/10.5771/2193-0147-2020-1-38
Grant, A. M. (2007). Relational job design and the motivation to make a prosocial difference. *Academy of Management Review, 32*, 393–417.
Grant, A. M. (2012). Giving time, time after time: Work design and sustained employee participation in corporate volunteering. *Academy of Management Review, 37*, 589–615.
Grube, J. A., & Piliavin, J. A. (2000). Role identity, organizational experiences, and volunteer performance. *Personality and Social Psychology Bulletin, 26*, 1108–1119.
Güntert, S. T. (2007). *Freiwilligenarbeit als Tätigsein in Organisationen*. Zentrum für Organisations- und Arbeitswissenschaften.

References

Hackman, J. R., & Oldham, G. R. (1976). Motivation through the design of work: Test of a theory. *Organizational Behavior and Human Performance, 16*, 250–279.

Haivas, S., Hofmans, J., & Pepermans, R. (2012). Self-determination theory as a framework for exploring the impact of the organizational context on volunteer motivation. *Nonprofit and Voluntary Sector Quarterly, 41*, 1195–1214.

Maas, S. A., Meijs, L. C. P. M., & Brudney, J. L. (2021). Designing "National Day of service" projects to promote volunteer job satisfaction. *Nonprofit and Voluntary Sector Quarterly, 50*(1), 089976402098266. https://doi.org/10.1177/0899764020982664

Mathou, C. (2010). *Volunteering in the European Union*. GHK.

McBey, K., Karakowsky, L., & Ng, P. (2017). Can I make a difference here? The impact of perceived organizational support on volunteer commitment. *Journal of Management Development, 36*(8), 991–1007.

Millette, V., & Gagné, M. (2008). Designing volunteers' tasks to maximize motivation, satisfaction and performance. *Motivation and Emotion, 32*, 11–22.

Nencini, A., Romaioli, D., & Meneghini, A. M. (2016). Volunteer motivation and organizational climate: Factors that promote satisfaction and sustained volunteerism in NPOs. *VOLUNTAS: International Journal of Voluntary and Nonprofit Organizations, 27*, 618–639.

Neufeind, M., Güntert, S. T., & Wehner, T. (2013). The impact of job design on event volunteers' future engagement. *European Sport Management Quarterly, 13*, 537–556.

Oostlander, J., Güntert, S. T., van Schie, S., & Wehner, T. (2014). Leadership and volunteer motivation: A study using self-determination theory. *Nonprofit and Voluntary Sector Quarterly, 43*, 869–889.

Penner, L. A. (2002). Dispositional and organizational influences on sustained volunteerism: An Interactionist perspective. *Journal of Social Issues, 58*, 447–467.

Piliavin, J. A., & Callero, P. L. (1991). *The Johns Hopkins series in contemporary medicine and public health. Giving blood: The development of an altruistic identity*. John Hopkins University Press.

Piliavin, J. A., Grube, J. A., & Callero, P. L. (2002). Role as resource for action in public service. *Journal of Social Issues, 58*, 469–485.

Posner, B. Z. (2015). An investigation into the leadership practices of volunteer leaders. *Leadership & Organization Development Journal, 36*(7), 885–898.

Stukas, A. A., Worth, K. A., Clary, E. G., & Snyder, M. (2009). The matching of motivations to affordances in the volunteer environment. *Nonprofit and Voluntary Sector Quarterly, 38*, 5–28.

Thoits, P. A. (2021). Motivations for peer-support volunteering: Social identities and role-identities as sources of motivation. *Nonprofit and Voluntary Sector Quarterly, 50*(4), 797–815. https://doi.org/10.1177/0899764020983897

van Schie, S., Gautier, A., Pache, A. C., & Güntert, S. T. (2019). What keeps corporate volunteers engaged: Extending the volunteer work design model with self-determination theory insights. *Journal of Business Ethics, 160*, 693–712.

van Schie, S., Güntert, S. T., & Wehner, T. (2014). How dare to demand this from volunteers! The impact of illegitimate tasks. *VOLUNTAS: International Journal of Voluntary and Nonprofit Organizations, 25*, 851–868.

van Schie, S., Güntert, S. T., & Wehner, T. (2015). Gestaltung von Aufgaben und organisationalen Rahmenbedingungen in der Freiwilligenarbeit. In T. Wehner & S. T. Güntert (Eds.), *Psychologie der Freiwilligenarbeit* (pp. 131–149). Springer.

Vecina, M. L., Chacòn, F., & Sueiro, M. J. (2010). Differences and similarities among volunteers who drop out during the first year and volunteers who continue after eight years. *The Spanish Journal of Psychology, 31*, 343–352.

Weinstein, N., & Ryan, R. M. (2010). When helping helps: Autonomous motivation for prosocial behavior and its influence on well-being for the helper and recipient. *Journal of Personality and Social Psychology, 98*(2), 222–244.

Yarnal, C. M., Dowler, L., & Hutchinson, S. (2004). Don't let the bastards see you sweat: Masculinity, public and private space, and the volunteer firehouse. *Environment and Planning A, 36*(4), 685–699.

Zaccaro, S. J., Ely, K., & Nelson, J. (2008). Leadership processes and work motivation. In R. Kanfer, G. Chen, & R. D. Pritchard (Eds.), *Work motivation: Past, present, and future* (pp. 319–360). Routledge.

Open Access This chapter is licensed under the terms of the Creative Commons Attribution 4.0 International License (http://creativecommons.org/licenses/by/4.0/), which permits use, sharing, adaptation, distribution and reproduction in any medium or format, as long as you give appropriate credit to the original author(s) and the source, provide a link to the Creative Commons license and indicate if changes were made.

The images or other third party material in this chapter are included in the chapter's Creative Commons license, unless indicated otherwise in a credit line to the material. If material is not included in the chapter's Creative Commons license and your intended use is not permitted by statutory regulation or exceeds the permitted use, you will need to obtain permission directly from the copyright holder.

Chapter 4
Volunteering as a Psychosocial Resource

It may seem paradoxical that working without remuneration can contribute to well-being, yet this is precisely what has been observed in empirical studies: Volunteer work can act as a *psychosocial resource*. In order to understand this rationale, it is important to see volunteering within the context of the salutogenic model and role theories. This helps explain how volunteering can:

- Contribute to maintaining health and promoting well-being.
- Complement or compensate other areas of activity, especially paid employment.
- Contribute to a better work–life balance.

4.1 The Salutogenic Approach to Volunteering and Health

The term *salutogenesis* was first coined by Aaron Antonovsky (1979) and is a framework that stands in stark contrast to the traditional, pathogenic approach to health and medicine. Whereas pathogenesis focuses on what makes individuals ill, salutogenesis delves into factors that help them thrive, even in the face of adversity. Such factors are primarily of the psychosocial type, where the different environments a person navigates play a key role. In sum, psychosocial resources can be defined as the individual differences and interpersonal characteristics of the environment that have beneficial effects on mental and physical health outcomes (Taylor & Broffman, 2011). At the core of the salutogenic model stands the concept of *sense of coherence* and its three pillars (Antonovsky, 1987): This is the idea that stress reduction and health promotion can be achieved when our environments are perceived as structured and predictable (*comprehensibility*), we feel capable to meet the demands posed by the environment (*manageability*), and these demands are seen as challenges worthy of our effort (*meaningfulness*). The salutogenic model has ignited

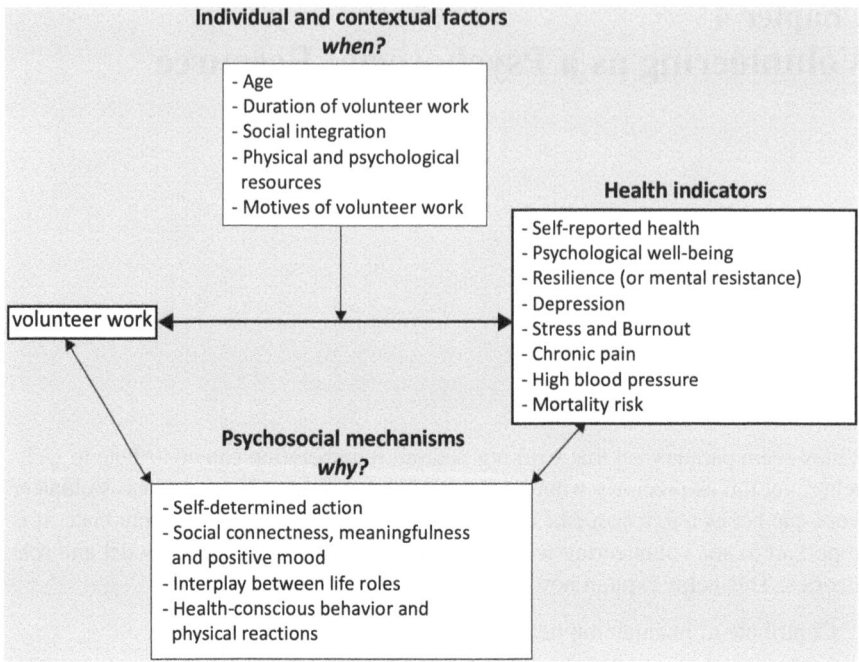

Fig. 4.1 Illustrating the context and causal factors for volunteer work and health. The double arrows leave the direction of causality open, i.e., bidirectional influences are considered. Single arrows indicate how contextual factors influence the relationship between volunteer work and health. (Source: Figure 7.1 from Ramos & Wehner, 2015)

new interest in recent years (Bauer et al., 2020), and the link between sense of coherence and health/well-being has found empirical support (Eriksson, 2017).

It is therefore clear that volunteering can be seen as a psychosocial resource from a salutogenic perspective: As a self-determined activity, we expect volunteers to experience a sense of control/autonomy over their tasks and meaningfulness in their engagement. Interpersonal characteristics, such as feedback, recognition, and social support, translate into enhanced individual factors such as a sense of competency, mastery, and belongingness, all of which strengthen an individual's psychosocial resources.

However, the relationship between volunteering and well-being is far from being a linear one. Whereas some factors serve as psychosocial mechanisms that explain *how* and *why* this relationship exists, certain individual and contextual factors explain *when*, or under which circumstances, volunteering and well-being are correlated. Figure 4.1 provides an overview of the different mediating and moderating factors considered in the scientific literature. We hereby provide some empirical evidence based primarily on longitudinal studies reported in Ramos and Wehner (2015), as well as more recent studies.

4.1 The Salutogenic Approach to Volunteering and Health

Psychosocial mechanisms: Why, or how, is volunteering associated with health and well-being? The central explanatory approach is found in the aforementioned salutogenic approach as well as in the theory of self-determination, which has been previously presented in connection with the motives of volunteer work (Sect. 2.3). Weinstein and Ryan (2010), for example, have laid out a multi-method series of studies that show how self-determined autonomous prosocial behavior can influence well-being for both the helper and the recipient. In addition to self-determination theory (see Sect. 2.3) and salutogenesis, the *role-enhancement* thesis (Greenhaus & Powell, 2006; Grzywacz & Marks, 2000) provides a framework for how the volunteer role can spillover to other domains, compensating or complementing other life roles. Some of the key findings for mediating effects are (cf. Ramos & Wehner, 2015):

- Volunteering can lead to *social connectedness* and a sense of belonging, which in turn can mitigate depressive symptoms, according to longitudinal studies (Musick & Wilson, 2003; Russell et al., 2019).
- Studies have shown that volunteering can bring about a sense of *meaningfulness* in our actions and the feeling that "our work matters." This, in turn, translates into psychological well-being and improved self-rated health (e.g., Piliavin & Siegl, 2007). Recognition from others further underscores that sense of meaningfulness, yielding beneficial changes in well-being such as lower ratings in depressive symptoms and higher life satisfaction (Matthews & Nazroo, 2021).
- In the long run, volunteer work is associated with increased happiness, higher self-esteem, greater life satisfaction, and more successful accomplishment of tasks, which correlate with *positive mood*, and lead to higher self-esteem and life satisfaction (Thoits & Hewitt, 2001) and lower cardiovascular risk according to a randomized controlled trial (Schreier et al., 2013).
- Volunteers report higher satisfaction with their *marriage and family life* (Jirovec, 2005).
- Volunteer work correlates positively with *paid work engagement*, which in turn correlates with better work performance (Rodell, 2013).
- Older volunteers are more functional in other life domains and *less prone to depression* than non-volunteers of the same age (Lum & Lightfoot, 2005).
- Volunteers acquire better *coping* mechanisms for work and everyday life and build stronger social networks that enable them to deal successfully with their living conditions (Luoh & Herzog, 2002).

Individual and contextual factors: Under which circumstances does volunteering have a positive impact on health and well-being? As stated earlier, volunteering does not automatically equate to better health. In fact, recent studies have questioned this thesis, as they have found no causal effects for volunteering, e.g., when controlling for personality traits such as neuroticism (King et al., 2014) or in a sample of students doing community service (Whillans et al., 2016). Several individual and contextual factors have been studied within the field of volunteering and some have been discussed in Chap. 3. We now present some of the evidence on moderating factors as it pertains to health-related outcomes (cf. Ramos & Wehner, 2015):

- *Age of volunteers:* A consistent pattern observed in research is that older volunteers seem to benefit more in terms of health-related outcomes than younger volunteers (Chi et al., 2021; Grimm et al., 2007; Hansen et al., 2018; Kim & Pai, 2010; Van Willigen, 2000).
- *Duration of volunteering:* Continuous volunteering over longer period of time is more often associated with better health-related outcomes in comparison to sporadic or short-lived engagement (Jiang et al., 2020; Musick & Wilson, 2003; Parkinson et al., 2010).
- *Motives for volunteering:* Other-oriented volunteering is more often associated with better health outcomes such as social well-being, lower depression, and better overall mental health (Yeung et al., 2018) than when the motives are self-oriented. Konrath et al. (2012) even found a relationship between volunteering and mortality rate four years later, with volunteers living longer than non-volunteers, but only when their motives were other-oriented.
- *Social integration/Physical and psychological resources:* While the social integration experienced in volunteering can cultivate psychological well-being, it is also true that pre-existing individual differences in social, physical, and psychological resources can also impact the effect of volunteering on health. Piliavin and Siegl (2007), for instance, found that people with lower social integration at baseline benefited the most from volunteering. A recent study also found lower suicide risk for volunteers with good mental health at baseline, but not for those with poor mental health (Rosato et al., 2019). Finally, volunteers with chronic diseases reported higher emotional stability and resilience than non-volunteers or volunteers without chronic conditions.

4.2 The Interaction Between Paid Work and Volunteering

In agreement with Greenhaus and Powell (2006), we assume that people can benefit from different, complementary roles in different areas of life (see Brauchli & Wehner, 2015). This can be explained by different psychological assumptions.

- *Additive model*: This concept suggests that experiences from different areas of life have additive effects on our well-being: Volunteer work can contribute to happiness, well-being, and life satisfaction in addition to volunteer work and other important areas of life and social roles.
- *Buffer model*: This approach suggests that participation in different areas of life can have a mutual, stress-buffering effect: Voluntary work has a high potential for such a buffering effect because it acts as a source of satisfaction and well-being for those who carry it out.
- *Synergistic model*: This variant suggests that the experiences we gain in one area of life (volunteering, hobbies) can generate benefits in other areas of life (gainful employment) in the sense of a transfer of positive experiences.

Although role theories (Grzywacz & Marks, 2000) suggest that an increase in roles and areas of activity also leads to an increase in conflicts, we postulate that volunteer work has a rather positive overall effect in the interaction of different areas of life and see three reasons for this:

1. *Stress buffer potential:* Volunteer work can influence the perception of stressors. For example, in the course of volunteering, stressors in one's work or family environment may come to be considered as irrelevant, thereby having a reduced negative impact on health and well-being (Lazarus & Folkman, 1984). Mojza and Sonnentag (2010) also found that volunteers may perceive potentially stressful situations as less relevant.
2. *Resource development potential:* Through their volunteer work, individuals can build resources such as social support, self-efficacy, and self-confidence (Brauchli et al., 2012, 2017). Not only can these be transferred directly to other areas of life (Hobfoll, 2011), but they also help to deal with stressors.
3. *Recovery potential:* Persons involved in volunteer work may show increased resilience, recovering more easily from stressful situations by regenerating their depleted resources through activity in another area of interest (Sonnentag & Zijlstra, 2006).

4.3 Work–Life Balance

The recent decades are characterized by considerable changes in social, economic, and technological structures. This change means that significant areas of life such as work, family, friends, hobbies, and formal/informal volunteer work have to be reconciled (see, e.g., Greenhaus & Allen, 2010). According to Brauchli and Wehner (2015), reconciliation means that the various areas of life are more- or less strongly separated (segmentation) or integrated (integration) depending on personal needs, goals, and circumstances. These preferences are not mutually exclusive, but can be either more- or less-pronounced, depending on life circumstances. If we are successful in this, we often speak of *work–life balance*, even though this term is misleading, as it excludes "work" from life and provides little nuance as to what "life" means (e.g., hobbies, volunteering, education, etc.).

Volunteer work is expected to have a positive impact on other areas of life and thus make a significant contribution to work–life balance. Nevertheless, the possibility should be considered that volunteer work could also prove to be a burden. On this question, Ketterer (2011) interviewed volunteers in England without parental responsibilities. The compatibility of different areas of life is also of great importance for this group of people, and the following statements can be considered typical.

- "My ideal career would be to do my job three days a week, then maybe one day a week in consulting and another day volunteering. That would give me something like a balance."

- "I don't like to have too much to do and the feeling that I won't make it. But my volunteering alongside my work is something that I enjoy and it feels good."
- "As long as the volunteer work comes in a package, so that I can integrate it, know how much time I have left, and I can say when I will be at home, then it is okay."
- "I have to make sure that I don't think about my work when I go in there; that I have a separation between my professional and my private life. That's how I create that balance for myself."

Data from the Swiss Household Panel (FORS, n.d.) show that the additional role of volunteering appears to reduce rather than increase compatibility problems (Brauchli & Wehner, 2015). Looking at the overall picture, there is an *inverted U-shaped relationship* between work–life balance and the frequency with which volunteer work is carried out: Volunteer work is perceived to be most beneficial at a rate of one to three times per month; if the frequency is higher or lower, volunteering is perceived as less beneficial to work–life balance.

Using an online questionnaire, employees in Switzerland were surveyed and information was obtained on their work–life balance, the demands and resources of their volunteer work, and their state of health (Ramos & Wehner, 2015). The extent of volunteer work correlated positively with self-reported health, psychological well-being, and work commitment and negatively with stress and burnout. It is interesting to note that volunteers rate their work–life balance as better than non-volunteers, which is reflected in better health. In an online survey of 746 Swiss workers (264 of which were volunteers), Ramos et al. (2015) found further support for the notion that assuming additional roles does not equate with more conflict.

4.4 Event Volunteering, Voluntourism

To conclude our chapter on volunteering as a psychosocial resource, we want to draw attention to a new phenomenon where the line between work and vacation is blurred: event volunteering, voluntourism. Volunteers are increasingly looking for forms of engagement that fit their biographies, promise spectacular experiences, and address social problems that are "in" at the moment (Hustinx & Lammertyn, 2003). Therefore, volunteering becomes less predictable and loses continuity (cf. Safrit & Merrill, 2000). In particular, three developments toward new forms of volunteering can be observed.

1. *From continuous volunteering to episodic and event volunteering*: When people volunteer, they usually do so regularly and over a long period of time. This image of the "long-term volunteer" often obscures the fact that a considerable amount of volunteer work is done in one-off projects, at major events, and at local events.
2. *From local engagement to global voluntourism*: Rising incomes, growing mobility, and new communication possibilities made worldwide tourism a central

social phenomenon of the twentieth century. Since the 1980s, alternative forms of tourism have been developing, referred to as ecological, sustainable, or even "soft" depending on their orientation. One of the fastest-growing forms of alternative tourism is voluntourism. Voluntourism means the combination of tourist travel with volunteer work and usually takes place abroad.

3. *From stationary to virtual volunteering*: Within the last 10 years, the Internet has become a central place of information exchange, value creation, and social interaction. This raises the question of the extent to which prosocial behaviors of the "offline world" are translated into virtual forms or replaced by them (Sproull et al., 2005). The term "virtual volunteering" refers to forms of volunteering that are fully or partially mediated via the Internet (Ellis & Cravens, 2000).

Based on these preliminary considerations, we conducted two studies to investigate the motivation of *event volunteers*. The first was a large-scale event, the 2008 European Football Championships, and the second was a local, community-based event, the "Action 72 Hours." We used the Volunteer Functions Inventory (VFI) by Clary et al. (1998) to assess the motivation of the volunteers. We newly added the *experience function*. Instead, we omitted the protection function; so far, this function has not been found to be relevant in any study in the event context.

The "Action 72 Hours" is a social action by youth associations in Germany, Switzerland, and Austria, which took place in Switzerland for the second time in 2010. The participating action groups each chose or were given a charitable social, ecological, intercultural, or political task to solve (after a phase of preparation) on a specific date within 72 hours. In 2010. More than 28,000 children and young people were involved in these actions. We interviewed 321 group leaders of these actions before and after their involvement.

EURO 2008 was one of the biggest events in Switzerland in recent years. We surveyed 870 "Host City Volunteers" of the German-speaking venues in Switzerland. These volunteers were mainly deployed for public viewing, traffic services, and guest services.

Figure 4.2 shows the importance of the different functions of volunteering for volunteers at the EURO 2008 tournament and the "Action 72 Hours." For comparison, where collected, the values of traditional volunteers of the Swiss Red Cross (525 respondents, mean age 47 years) and Amnesty International Switzerland (285 respondents, mean age 48 years) are given. The reported differences are statistically significant.

First of all, it becomes apparent that the *experience* function is the most important function or motivation for event volunteers. For classic volunteers involved with Amnesty International, on the other hand, it hardly plays a role. The social adaptation function, on the other hand, plays a clearly weaker role for EURO 2008 volunteers than for classic Red Cross volunteers. The commitment of friends and relatives, and the pressure to do the same, thus seems to be a less important motive for volunteering at major events. Interestingly, among the volunteers of the local event "Action 72 Hours," a manifestation of the social adaptation function is found,

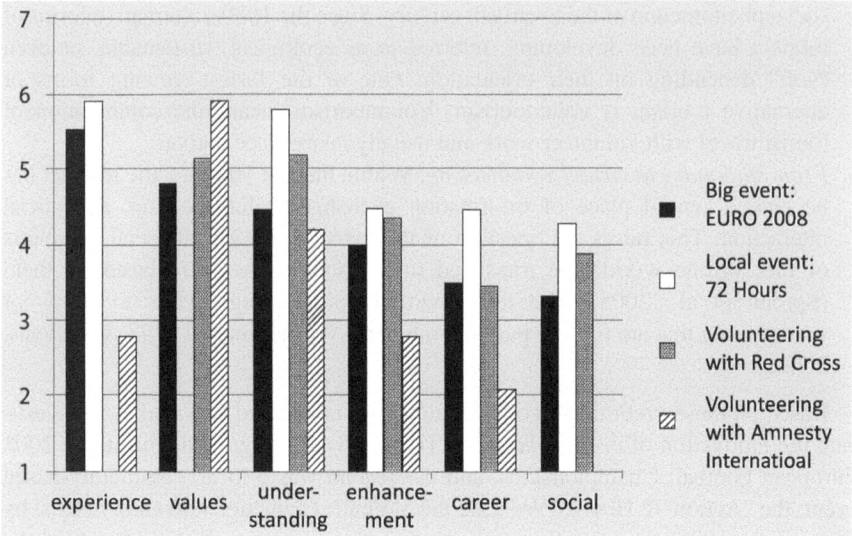

Fig. 4.2 Comparison of the importance of the functions of volunteering (cf. Clary et al., 1998) among event volunteers and classic volunteers

which is even higher than that among classical volunteers. One explanation may be that volunteers involved in "Action 72 Hours" or similar initiatives have a very high attachment to their community. Interestingly, career considerations are not generally more pronounced among event volunteers. Volunteering had a particularly strong career function for the group leaders of the "Action 72 Hours."

In addition to the question of *why* (i.e., motivation), psychological research into voluntary work is increasingly concerned with the question of *what*, i.e., the design and organization of voluntary work. Even though volunteer work is not gainful employment, since it is unpaid, it is still work in the sense that it could be paid under other circumstances. Therefore, in our survey of EURO 2008 volunteers, we also recorded the five job characteristics specified in Hackman and Oldham's (1976) Job Characteristics Model. All reported differences are statistically significant.

Figure 4.3 shows that the design of the volunteer activities at the EURO 2008 across all activity characteristics turns out to be *less motivating* than in activities that are usually found in gainful employment. Compared to traditional volunteer work, the activities at EURO 2008 are also less well designed, with the exception of the diversity dimension. However, there is a large variance between the activities. The volunteers who worked in the so-called Fan Embassies (information and help for visitors to the EURO 2008 tournament) report a very motivating activity design, while the volunteers in the Parking task area report a very less motivating activity design.

But is the design of volunteer activities at all significant for event volunteers? Studies in the context of classic volunteering have shown that the design of volunteer activities has an influence on the satisfaction of volunteers and their willingness to

4.4 Event Volunteering, Voluntourism

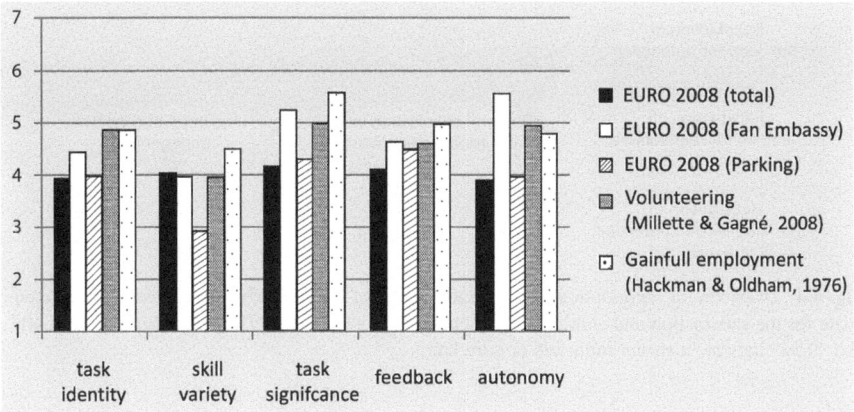

Fig. 4.3 Comparison of activity characteristics according to Hackman and Oldham (1976) for event volunteering, traditional volunteering, and gainful employment

remain involved. Studies of this nature have been scarce for event-based volunteering (Doherty, 2009). Therefore, in our analysis of volunteering at EURO 2008, we also investigated which activity characteristics could be considered success factors. For this purpose, hierarchical regression analyses were conducted, as presented in Neufeind et al. (2013). First, it was shown that *activity characteristics have a significant influence on volunteer satisfaction in the event context as well.* A good 37% of the variance in satisfaction could be explained.

The character of volunteering as an experience emerges strongly when we consider *voluntourism*. Every year, tens of thousands of people, most of them young, travel abroad to do volunteer work in social institutions, agricultural initiatives, or nature reserves. We see a new form of volunteering emerging here: Voluntourism. There are already some findings on the motivation of voluntourists. In one of the first studies, conducted by Rehberg (2005), people who had inquired at Caritas Switzerland and the Center for Information, Counseling, and Education (cinfo) about possible short-term assignments abroad, i.e., who were potential volunteers, were asked about their motivation. Rehberg identified 12 motives, which were assigned to three groups:

1. To achieve something positive for others. This group includes the motives of helping, wanting to bring about change, wanting to realize ethical values, and feeling useful.
2. Striving for something new. This group includes the motives of seeking intercultural exchange, the desire for variety, becoming familiar with a new culture, contact as well as learning and expanding language skills.
3. The search for the self. This group includes the motives of personality development, discovering and exceeding personal limits, and wanting to develop professionally.

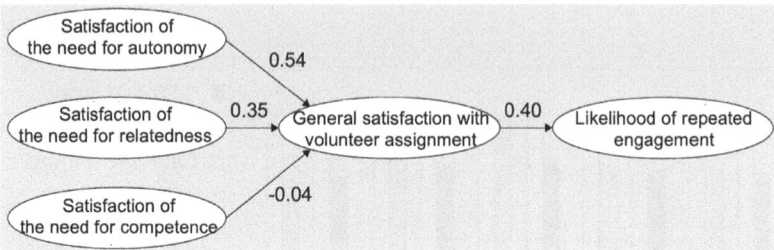

Fig. 4.4 Overview of regression analyses: Satisfaction of basic psychological needs as a prerequisite for the satisfaction and continuation intention of voluntourists. The numbers "0.35," "0.40," and "0.54" indicate a strong influence or correlation

Hudson and Inkson (2006) found a similar mix of altruism, adventurousness, and self-actualization.

As part of Kuhn's (2013) study, 54 Germans and Swiss individuals who had volunteered abroad as part of "Service Civil International" (SCI) during the previous three years were asked to complete Clary et al.'s (1998) VFI. Within this framework, we also examined the extent to which the fulfillment of the three basic psychological needs (Ryan & Deci, 2000) in the context of self-determination theory (i.e., the needs for autonomy, competence, and relationship during engagement) determined volunteers' overall satisfaction with their engagement as well as their likelihood of repeated engagement. Regression analyses showed that in our sample of voluntourists, *fulfillment of the needs for autonomy and relationship had a significant impact on volunteers' overall satisfaction* (see Fig. 4.4). However, the fulfillment of the need for competence had no influence.

References

Antonovsky, A. (1979). *Health, stress, and coping. New perspectives on mental and physical wellbeing* (pp. 12–37). Jossey-Bass.
Antonovsky, A. (1987). *Unraveling the mystery of health: How people manage stress and stay well.* Jossey-Bass.
Bauer, G. F., Roy, M., Bakibinga, P., Contu, P., Downe, S., Eriksson, M., Espnes, G. A., Jensen, B. B., Canal, D. J., Lindström, B., Mana, A., Mittelmark, M. B., Morgan, A. R., Pelikan, J. M., Saboga-Nunes, L., Sagy, S., Shorey, S., Vaandrager, L., & Vinje, H. F. (2020). Future directions for the concept of salutogenesis: A position article. *Health Promotion International, 35*(2), 187–195.
Brauchli, R., Hämmig, O., Güntert, S., Bauer, G. F., & Wehner, T. (2012). Vereinbarkeit von Erwerbsarbeit und Privatleben: Freiwilligentätigkeit als psychosoziale Ressource. *Zeitschrift für Arbeits- und Organisationspsychologie, 56*(1), 24–36.
Brauchli, R., Peeters, M. C., Steenbergen, E. F., Wehner, T., & Hämmig, O. (2017). The work-home interface: Linking work-related wellbeing and volunteer work. *Journal of Community & Applied Social Psychology, 27*(1), 50–64.
Brauchli, R., & Wehner, T. (2015). Verbessert Freiwilligenarbeit die "Work-Life-Balance"? In T. Wehner & S. T. Güntert (Eds.), *Psychologie der Freiwilligenarbeit* (pp. 169–180). Springer.

References

Chi, K., Almeida, D. M., Charles, S. T., & Sin, N. L. (2021). Daily prosocial activities and well-being: Age moderation in two national studies. *Psychology and Aging, 36*(1), 83.

Clary, E. G., Snyder, M., Ridge, R. D., Copeland, J., Stukas, A. A., Haugen, J., & Miene, P. (1998). Understanding and assessing the motivations of volunteers. *Journal of Personality and Social Psychology, 74*, 1516–1530.

Doherty, A. (2009). The volunteer legacy of a major sport event. *Journal of Policy Research in Tourism, Leisure and Events, 1*(3), 185–207.

Ellis, S. J., & Cravens, J. (2000). *The virtual volunteering guidebook*. Impact Online.

Eriksson, M. (2017). The sense of coherence in the salutogenic model of health. In M. B. Mittelmark, S. Sagy, M. Eriksson, G. F. Bauer, J. M. Pelikan, B. Lindström, & G. A. Espnes (Eds.), *The handbook of salutogenesis* (pp. 91–96). Springer.

FORS. (n.d.). *Swiss household panel*. https://forscenter.ch/projects/swiss-household-panel.

Greenhaus, J. H., & Allen, T. D. (2010). Work-family balance: A review and extension of the literature. In J. C. Quick & L. E. Tetrick (Eds.), *Handbook of occupational health psychology* (2nd ed., pp. 165–183). APA.

Greenhaus, J. H., & Powell, G. N. (2006). When work and family are allies: A theory of work-family enrichment. *Academy of Management Review, 31*, 72–92.

Grimm, R., Spring, K., & Dietz, N. (2007). *The health benefits of volunteering: A review of recent research*. Corporation for National & Community Service.

Grzywacz, J. G., & Marks, N. F. (2000). Reconceptualizing the work-family interface. *Journal of Occupational Health Psychology, 5*, 111–126.

Hackman, J. R., & Oldham, G. R. (1976). Motivation through the design of work: Test of a theory. *Organizational Behavior and Human Performance, 16*, 250–279.

Hansen, T., Aartsen, M., Slagsvold, B., & Deindl, C. (2018). Dynamics of volunteering and life satisfaction in midlife and old age: Findings from 12 European countries. *Social Sciences, 7*(5), 78.

Hobfoll, S. E. (2011). Conservation of resource caravans and engaged settings. *Journal of Occupational and Organizational Psychology, 84*, 116–122.

Hudson, S., & Inkson, K. (2006). Volunteer overseas development workers: The hero's adventure and personal transformation. *Career Development International, 11*(4), 304–320.

Hustinx, L., & Lammertyn, F. (2003). Collective and reflexive styles of volunteering: A sociological modernization perspective. *VOLUNTAS: International Journal of Voluntary and Nonprofit Organizations, 14*(2), 167–187.

Jiang, D., Warner, L. M., Chong, A. M. L., Li, T., Wolff, J. K., & Chou, K. L. (2020). Benefits of volunteering on psychological well-being in older adulthood: Evidence from a randomized controlled trial. *Aging & Mental Health, 25*(4), 641–649.

Jirovec, R. L. (2005). Differences in family functioning and health between older adult volunteers and non-volunteers. *Journal of Gerontological Social Work, 46*(2), 23–35.

Ketterer, H. (2011). *Work-life balance among young adults in full-time employment and engaged in formal volunteering in Cambridgeshire* [Master thesis accepted at the University of Cambridge].

Kim, J., & Pai, M. (2010). Volunteering and trajectories of depression. *Journal of Aging and Health, 22*, 84–105.

King, H. R., Jackson, J. J., Morrow-Howell, N., & Oltmanns, T. F. (2014). Personality accounts for the connection between volunteering and health. *Journals of Gerontology Series B: Psychological Sciences and Social Sciences, 70*, 691–697.

Konrath, S., Fuhrel-Forbis, A., Lou, A., & Brown, S. (2012). Motives for volunteering are associated with mortality risk in older adults. *Health Psychology, 31*(1), 87–96.

Kuhn, C. (2013). *Motive und Bedürfnisse von Volunteer Tourists: Freiwilligenarbeit im Ausland zwischen Hilfe und Ferien* [Unpublished Bachelor's thesis at Zürcher Hochschule für Angewandte Wissenschaften]. http://www.zhaw.ch/fileadmin/user_upload/psychologie/Downloads/Bibliothek/Arbeiten/BA/ba0234.pdf

Lazarus, R. L., & Folkman, S. (1984). *Stress, appraisal, and coping*. Springer.

Lum, T. Y., & Lightfoot, E. (2005). The effects of volunteering on the physical and mental health of older people. *Research on Aging, 27*(1), 31–55.

Luoh, M.-C., & Herzog, R. A. (2002). Individual consequences of volunteer and paid work in old age: Health and mortality. *Journal of Health and Social Behavior, 43*, 490–509.

Matthews, K., & Nazroo, J. (2021). The impact of volunteering and its characteristics on well-being after state pension age: Longitudinal evidence from the English longitudinal study of ageing. *The Journals of Gerontology: Series B, 76*(3), 632–641.

Millette, V., & Gagné, M. (2008). Designing volunteers' tasks to maximize motivation, satisfaction and performance. *Motivation and Emotion, 32*, 11–22.

Mojza, E. J., & Sonnentag, S. (2010). Does volunteer work during leisure time buffer negative effects of job stressors? *European Journal of Work and Organizational Psychology, 19*(2), 231–252. https://doi.org/10.1080/13594320902986097

Musick, M. A., & Wilson, J. (2003). Volunteering and depression: The role of psychological and social resources in different age groups. *Social Science & Medicine, 56*(2), 259–269.

Neufeind, M., Güntert, S. T., & Wehner, T. (2013). The impact of job design on event volunteers' future engagement. *European Sport Management Quarterly, 13*, 537–556.

Parkinson, L., Warburton, J., Sibbritt, S., & Byles, J. (2010). Volunteering and older women: Psychosocial and health predictors of participation. *Aging and Mental Health, 14*, 917–927.

Piliavin, J. A., & Siegl, E. (2007). Health benefits of volunteering in the Wisconsin longitudinal study. *Journal of Health and Social Behavior, 48*(4), 450–464.

Ramos, R., & Wehner, T. (2015). Hält Freiwilligenarbeit gesund? Erklärungsansätze und kontextuelle Faktoren. In T. Wehner & S. T. Güntert (Eds.), *Psychologie der Freiwilligenarbeit* (pp. 109–127). Springer.

Ramos, R., Brauchli, R., Bauer, G., Wehner, T., & Hämmig, O. (2015). Busy yet socially engaged: Volunteering, work–life balance, and health in the working population. *Journal of Occupational and Environmental Medicine, 57*(2), 164–172.

Rehberg, W. (2005). Altruistic individualists: Motivations for international volunteering among young adults in Switzerland. *Voluntas: International Journal of Voluntary and Nonprofit Organizations, 16*(2), 109–122.

Rodell, J. B. (2013). Finding meaning through volunteering: Why do employees volunteer and what does it mean for their jobs? *Academy of Management Journal, 56*(5), 1274–1294.

Rosato, M., Tseliou, F., Wright, D. M., Maguire, A., & O'Reilly, D. (2019). Are volunteering and care giving associated with suicide risk? A census-based longitudinal study. *BMC Psychiatry, 19*(1), 1–10.

Russell, A. R., Nyame-Mensah, A., de Wit, A., & Handy, F. (2019). Volunteering and wellbeing among ageing adults: A longitudinal analysis. *Voluntas: International Journal of Voluntary and Nonprofit Organizations, 30*(1), 115–128.

Ryan, R. M., & Deci, E. L. (2000). The darker and brighter sides of human existence: Basic psychological needs as a unifying concept. *Psychological Inquiry, 11*(4), 319–338.

Safrit, R. D., & Merrill, M. (2000). Management implications of contemporary trends in voluntarism in the United States and Canada. *Voluntary Action, 3*(1), 73–88.

Schreier, H. M., Schonert-Reichl, K. A., & Chen, E. (2013). Effect of volunteering on risk factors for cardiovascular disease in adolescents: A randomized controlled trial. *JAMA Pediatrics, 167*(4), 327–332.

Sonnentag, S., & Zijlstra, F. R. H. (2006). Job characteristics and off-job activities as predictors of need for recovery, well-being, and fatigue. *Journal of Applied Psychology, 91*, 330–350.

Sproull, L., Conley, C., & Moon, J. Y. (2005). Prosocial behavior on the net. In Y. Amichai-Hamburger (Ed.), *The social net: Understanding human behavior in cyberspace* (pp. 139–161). Oxford University Press.

Taylor, S. E., & Broffman, J. I. (2011). Psychosocial resources: Functions, origins, and links to mental and physical health. In *Advances in experimental social psychology* (Vol. 44, pp. 1–57). Academic Press.

References

Thoits, P. A., & Hewitt, L. N. (2001). Volunteer work and well-being. *Journal of Health and Social Behavior, 42*, 115–131.

Van Willigen, M. (2000). Differential benefits of volunteering across the life course. *Journals of Gerontology – Series B Psychological Sciences and Social Sciences, 55*(5), S308–S318.

Weinstein, N., & Ryan, R. M. (2010). When helping helps: Autonomous motivation for prosocial behavior and its influence on well-being for the helper and recipient. *Journal of Personality and Social Psychology, 98*(2), 222–244.

Whillans, A. V., Seider, S. C., Chen, L., Dwyer, R. J., Novick, S., Gramigna, K. J., Mitchell, B. A., Savalei, V., Dickerson, S. S., & Dunn, E. W. (2016). Does volunteering improve well-being? *Comprehensive Results in Social Psychology, 1*(1–3), 35–50.

Yeung, J. W., Zhang, Z., & Kim, T. Y. (2018). Volunteering and health benefits in general adults: Cumulative effects and forms. *BMC Public Health, 18*(1), 1–8.

Open Access This chapter is licensed under the terms of the Creative Commons Attribution 4.0 International License (http://creativecommons.org/licenses/by/4.0/), which permits use, sharing, adaptation, distribution and reproduction in any medium or format, as long as you give appropriate credit to the original author(s) and the source, provide a link to the Creative Commons license and indicate if changes were made.

The images or other third party material in this chapter are included in the chapter's Creative Commons license, unless indicated otherwise in a credit line to the material. If material is not included in the chapter's Creative Commons license and your intended use is not permitted by statutory regulation or exceeds the permitted use, you will need to obtain permission directly from the copyright holder.

Chapter 5
Volunteer Work from an International Perspective

Those who volunteer do so for individual motives. A particular volunteering activity may be undertaken for a range of individual motives. At the same time, some motives are more important for commitment than others if we compare one and the same volunteer activity and volunteers with the same socio-demographic background across countries. How can this be explained? In this chapter, we will look at societal factors that can influence individual motives for volunteering (cf. Neufeind et al., 2015).

The French politician and publicist Alexis de Tocqueville, visiting the still young the USA, observed that Americans of all ages, ranks, and walks of life were constantly coming together; wherever you would see the government in France and a great gentleman at the head in England, you would certainly find a civic grouping in the USA (Neufeind et al., 2015, p. 266). After returning to post-revolutionary France in the early nineteenth century, de Tocqueville wrote his famous work *De la démocratieen Amérique* (Democracy in America, cf. de Tocqueville, 1835/2002), describing how the form and extent of civil society differed between countries. This is still true today: More than 40% of adults in the USA or Sweden are engaged in volunteer work, while in Spain or Lithuania, the figure is less than 20% (Hodgkinson, 2003).

How can these differences be explained? When trying to predict whether a person will volunteer, reference is usually made to factors at the individual level. The higher their socioeconomic status; the greater the involvement of family, friends, and acquaintances; the more pronounced the motivation or sense of justice; the more likely it is that a person will volunteer. In addition, various theoretical approaches, broadly categorized as *cultural* or *structural*, are applied to explain inter-country differences. Cultural approaches emphasize values and principles that prevail in certain cultures but not in others. Structural approaches emphasize the economic, social, and political structures of a country.

© The Author(s) 2022
S. T. Güntert et al., *Organizational, Motivational, and Cultural Contexts of Volunteering*, SpringerBriefs in Psychology,
https://doi.org/10.1007/978-3-030-92817-9_5

5.1 Structural Approaches

Structural approaches examine, above all, the connection between social institutions and the altruistic and career-related motivation for engagement.

5.1.1 Social Welfare and Altruistic Motivation

Comparing and Canada and the USA, Hwang et al. (2005) found that US volunteers were more altruistically motivated, whereas their Canadian counterparts expressed more self-referential motives. Hwang et al. (2005) argue that although both countries are liberal democracies, Canada is characterized by a more comprehensive welfare state (such as universal access to public health care). Therefore, Americans see it as part of their role as citizens to help poorer and disadvantaged fellow citizens, while Canadians see this role as largely fulfilled by the welfare state. Consequently, this would also explain the more altruistic motives of US volunteers. When comparing countries at different levels of economic development (Bangladesh, Ghana, Poland, and South Korea), Ziemek (2006) came to a similar conclusion: In countries with established social welfare, altruistic motivation was less pronounced.

Based on these results and the Social Origins Theory (cf. Salamon & Anheier, 1998), Hustinx et al. (2010) formulated the thesis that volunteers are altruistically motivated above all when they provide social services that are not provided by the state. Consequently, one should find strong altruistic motivation, especially in "liberal" countries like the UK or the USA, medium altruistic motivation in corporatist countries like France or Germany, and weak altruistic motivation in social democratic countries like Norway or Sweden. Hustinx et al. (2010) were able to confirm these assumptions empirically: In their study, Belgian, Chinese, and Japanese students who volunteered reported significantly lower altruistic motivation than Canadian and US students. By expanding the sample to 12 countries, the research group (Handy et al., 2010) was able to confirm the results once again. Students in corporatist or "statist" countries (Belgium, China, India, Japan, the Netherlands) showed lower altruistic motivation than those in liberal countries (Canada, UK, USA).

5.1.2 Signal Value and Career Motivation

Often, the motives of volunteers have something to do with the person of the volunteer(s). One motive is to gain career-relevant experience and to open up professional opportunities through the volunteering experience. There is ample evidence that volunteering is "worthwhile" in this sense: People who volunteer have higher salaries and both better jobs and better career prospects (Day & Devlin,

1998; Freeman, 1997; Katz & Rosenberg, 2005; Menchik & Weisbrod, 1987; Prouteau & Wolff, 2006). One explanation for the professional success of volunteers is that volunteering "signals" desirable characteristics to potential employers (according to the Job Market Signaling theory by Spence, 1973). For example, volunteering as a member of an association's board of directors signals organizational and communicative skills that can be of great relevance in the position of project manager or team leader. It can be assumed that in many volunteer activities, general skills can be acquired that are also applicable in a gainful employment context (Strauß, 2009).

The signal value of volunteer work differs between countries. In countries where extracurricular experience and general skills are important recruitment criteria, the signal value of volunteering should be high, and career considerations should be an important motive. Hustinx et al. (2010) showed that volunteers in the USA and Canada, where volunteering has a high signal value, have stronger career motivation than volunteers in Belgium, Finland, and Japan, where volunteering has a low signal value. In an extended sample, the research group (Handy et al., 2010) confirmed these results: In Canada, the UK, and USA, career motivation was significantly higher than in Finland, Japan, and Korea.

We therefore believe it makes sense, following Strauß (2009), to consider characteristics of the market economy framework as relevant structural factors. In particular, two factors should play a role: First, the signal value of volunteering should depend on *how often* volunteers can use their volunteering experience to signal desired characteristics (i.e., labor market flexibility). Secondly, the signal value of volunteering should depend on the *importance* of general cognitive and non-cognitive skills that can be signaled by volunteering. Both factors vary considerably between countries.

In "liberal market economies," such as the UK and USA, there is much greater labor market flexibility than in "coordinated market economies" such as Germany, Sweden, and Switzerland (Hall & Gingerich, 2009). Changes in career, employer, and phases of unemployment are more frequent in liberal market economies (Rubery & Grimshaw, 2003). In liberal market economies, employers "tend to take the risk of relying on non-certified skills," while in coordinated market economies "certified vocational training is the decisive signal for employers" (Strauß, 2009, p. 650). These differences are reflected both in the individual orientations of university graduates (Hoelscher, 2012) and in the effects that voluntary engagement has on the re-employment opportunities of the unemployed (Strauß, 2009).

5.2 Cultural Approaches

As to cultural approaches, the starting point is the assumption that countries differ in their cultural values. According to Schwartz (1999), cultural values are implicitly- or explicitly-shared abstract ideas about what is good, right, and desirable in a society. The extensive work of the social psychologists Hofstede (2001) and Schwartz

(1994) clearly shows that countries do indeed differ systematically with respect to these prevailing values. Dekker and Halman (2003) and Finkelstein (2011) argue that cultural values only conditionally determine whether a person volunteers or not, but that they have a strong influence on what motivates someone to volunteer. Grönlund et al. (2011) have attempted to explain country differences in motives for volunteering through cultural values. To provide an overview:

5.2.1 Egalitarianism and Altruistic Motive

From a structural perspective, differences in the altruistic motivation of volunteers can be explained by the existing or non-existing welfare state commitment of the country in which the volunteer is engaged. Grönlund et al. (2011) contrast this with the thesis that altruistic motivation is mainly found in egalitarian countries. Egalitarianism, in the sense of Schwartz (1994), means a socially shared norm of equality, responsibility, and helpfulness. In egalitarian societies, the individual is thus jointly responsible for the well-being of his fellow citizens. In an analysis of 13 countries, Grönlund et al. (2011) showed that in countries with high levels of egalitarianism, such as Finland, volunteers are more altruistically motivated. However, the altruistic motive was also strongly pronounced among respondents from Canada, New Zealand, and the USA, which is more in line with the structural considerations of the welfare state in the section on "Structural Approaches."

5.2.2 Individualism and Career Motive

The significance of the career motive for volunteers depends, among other things, on the signal value of volunteering to potential employers (see section on "Structural Approaches"). Cultural values could also explain differences: Grönlund et al. (2011) argue that in countries with a strong individualistic culture, career motives should be more important. In the sense of Hofstede (2001), individualism refers to the social desirability of self-determination, personal responsibility, and the pursuit of self-defined goals. A high degree of individualism can be found in the UK or USA, for example, and a low degree in China or Korea. Finkelstein (2011) was able to show on an individual level that individualistic volunteers show stronger career motivation. In their comparative study, Grönlund et al. (2011) found that career motivation is significantly stronger in individualistic countries. In contrast, especially in Finland, Japan, and Korea, this motive barely played any role for volunteers.

5.2.3 *Conservatism and the Motive of Social Adaptation*

Voluntary engagement is often promoted by the expectations of the social environment (for example, when family and friends also volunteer). In addition, individuals can strengthen their own integration into a group through volunteering. This function of volunteering is known as social adaptation. Grönlund et al. (2011) have suggested that the motive of social adaptation should be particularly important in conservative countries. According to Schwartz (1999), conservatism means that the existing—usually unequal—distribution of roles and resources is considered legitimate and that the individual must adapt to obligations and regulations. However, Grönlund et al. (2011) did not find a significant positive correlation between a country's conservatism and the importance of the motive of social adaptation.

5.2.4 *Affective Autonomy and Protective Motive*

Volunteering can distract from one's own worries, reduce feelings of loneliness, and relieve feelings of guilt that arise from the fact that one has it better than other people. If volunteers consider this function of their commitment to be particularly important, they have a strong protective motive. Grönlund et al. (2011) put forward the thesis that the motive for protection should be found particularly in countries where affective autonomy is important. According to Schwartz (1999), affective autonomy means that individuals are encouraged to have positive affective experiences and to lead exciting and varied lives. Schwartz (1999) found high values for affective autonomy, above all, in Anglo-Saxon countries and in Israel. In the study by Grönlund et al. (2011), the motive of protection was highly pronounced in Israel, but overall there was no significant connection between affective autonomy and the motive of protection.

5.2.5 *Intellectual Autonomy and Motive for Understanding*

For many people, volunteering is an opportunity to learn new things, pursue interests, gain practical experience, get to know a specific social environment, and, last but not least, to better understand themselves. This is termed the experiential motive. Analogous to the considerations of affective autonomy, Grönlund et al. (2011) assume that this motive for experience should be found particularly in countries where intellectual autonomy is important. Schwartz (1999) understands intellectual autonomy to mean that, in a society, the individual, independent pursuit of one's own ideas and ways of thinking is desired and that curiosity, flexibility in thinking, and creativity are positively sanctioned. Schwartz (1999) found high values for intellectual autonomy in Canada, the Netherlands, and French-speaking

Switzerland, for example. However, Grönlund et al. (2011) did not find a significant positive correlation between intellectual autonomy and the motive of experience.

> **The Swiss Militia System (cf. Ketterer et al., 2015)** The ways in which volunteering is embedded in distinct structural and cultural contexts can be illustrated by the case of Switzerland. Central to Swiss democracy is the idea of *self-government* vested in the so-called militia system, which institutionalizes citizens' participation in local politics and administration. According to Geser (1987, p. 16), the militia system can be seen as a form of "self-government:" it relies on citizens volunteering in political-administrative offices alongside their job duties. This arrangement ought to prevent the centralization of power, the formation of special interests, and the abuse of power (p. 17). Such a system fits into a decentralized federalism that originated from a small-scale and homogeneous polity in the Swiss *Alteidgenossenschaften* (confederations) in the thirteenth and fourteenth centuries.
>
> The original cells of the militia system are considered the *military service*, the *Landsgemeinde* (assembly of voters) and the *agricultural commons*. As the militia system was originally located in traditional communities organized around the cultivation of collectively owned land, it served the organization of community life not only politically but also economically. That is, citizens were mutually dependent on each other's voluntary engagement for the provision of security and material needs. For these reasons, citizens would gain recognition from other community members when participating in the militia system. However, with the development of modern capitalism and the introduction of wage labor, the traditional community has lost not only its economic function but also its importance as a primary source of recognition.
>
> In contrast to a board of professional experts, the *lay authority* created by the militia system represents the unity of state and society (Kussau et al., 2007). The militia system relies on the Helvetic virtue of citizen participation and on "opportunities for participation" created by the state and linked to citizenship (Kussau et al., 2007, p. 6). Kussau and Wehner (2007) also refer to the lay authority as a "paradoxical form of a non-voluntary participation necessity based on voluntary participation." However, it is not only Helvetic republicanism that characterizes Switzerland's political culture, but rather the interplay between republicanism and liberalism. In the militia system, these two opposing ideational currents clash in a sensitive way: republican virtues rub up against liberal value orientations. If one understands participation in shaping the community as a republican civic virtue, it requires Swiss citizens not only to fulfill their rights at the ballot box on election or voting day, but also to commit themselves in the form of regular, active participation in the *res publica*. In contrast, liberal value orientations free citizens from normative regulation, including from the duty of political participation.

(continued)

In a comparative study on volunteers' motives for participating in militia offices in municipalities, churches, and schools across the canton of Zürich, Ketterer et al. (2015) find that *both other-oriented and self-enhancing motives matter for participation*. Citizens volunteer their time because they want to do a service to the local community, but also because they aim to shape local affairs and want to do an activity that is meaningful to them personally. Further, the findings highlight that participation is also perceived as a moral obligation to the community.

Recently, the militia system has come under increased criticism, *as militia offices in many municipalities remain unfilled or have been abandoned due to resignations* (see, for example, Freitag et al., 2019; Kussau & Wehner, 2007). Every other municipality reports difficulties in finding candidates (Ladner et al., 2013). However, from the available data, it is difficult to assess the extent of the crisis that has been identified: Since the beginnings of municipal monitoring in the 1980s, there have been continuous reports of difficulties experienced by municipalities in finding suitable candidates for advertised militia offices (Ladner et al., 2013). Yet, research suggests that the issue of vacancies and uncontested elections has worsened over time. Dlabac et al. (2014) show for the German-speaking northern canton of Aargau that this problem has increased over time and particularly affects small, rural municipalities. In view of this problem of unfilled civic posts, institutional reform, constitutional changes (abolition of the school board, for example, in the canton of Aargau), and pressures for professionalization, the future of the lay authority is increasingly uncertain. In this context, the think tank "Avenir Suisse" also speaks of the "crisis of the militia system" (Müller, 2013) and proposes *a universal civic service* that would be obligatory for Swiss citizens and non-citizens with permanent residence in Switzerland.

Meanwhile, the issue of non-participation remains central to public discourse, with various assumptions about lack of engagement in the militia system attributed to *tensions between modern lifestyles and a traditional commitment*. Research, however, suggests examining a number of factors to explain non-participation both at the individual (e.g., age, gender) and organizational (e.g., strategic vs. operative task, support of employer) levels, but also at the structural level (Freitag et al., 2019). With regard to structural factors, the literature points to *increased demands concerning qualification and commitment* (Dlabac, 2016). Furthermore, difficulties should also be seen in the context of declining political participation at the municipal level and a decrease in party members overall (cf. Kriesi & Trechsel, 2008). As a result, where once potential candidates had been nominated by fellow party members, municipal councils today are *increasingly nonpartisan*. For example, in school boards less than 60% of militia members are members of a political party.

(continued)

> Nevertheless, self-reported data seem to support public discourse on a number of issues. From the perspective of those volunteering in municipalities, difficulties arise from the time-intensity of the commitment, the issue of balancing professional and private life (Ladner, 2015), and a lack of public and social recognition of the militia service (Freitag et al., 2019; Ketterer et al., 2015; Ladner, 2015). Hence, commitment to the local community appears *no longer compatible with the opportunities and demands of a modern, globalized working world*, which has undermined the unity of economic and political life as it existed in the traditional community.

5.3 Cultural and Structural Differences: Volunteer Work at the Red Cross in Europe

In a cross-national study (cf. Neufeind, 2013), we applied structural and cultural approaches to explain differences in motives for volunteering in eight European countries. Our data originated from a large survey of more than 6000 Red Cross volunteers in Austria, France, Germany, Italy, Lithuania, Spain, Sweden, and Switzerland, which we conducted in 2012. The sample consisted of first aid volunteers (32%), social services volunteers (55%), and administrative or supportive volunteers (13%). The eight sample countries differ with regard to several welfare, labor, and civil society characteristics (see Table 5.1) which we assumed to affect motives to volunteer, building upon the existing literature outline above. We particularly focused on aspects of the *labor market* and *work organization* in the realm of paid employment, such as discretion or workload, as well as citizenship norms and attitudes.

Five hypotheses were tested (using multiple regression analysis and controlling for gender, age, occupation, volunteer job, household income, paid work hours, and volunteer work hours):

1. Following Social Origins Theory (Salamon & Anheier, 1998), *volunteers in countries with low social protection should report higher motivation by altruistic values than volunteers in countries with high social protection.* In line with this hypothesis, we found the highest level of values-motivation to be reported by volunteers in countries with the lowest per capita social spending (Lithuania and Spain), while in countries with high per capita social spending (Switzerland and Austria), the lowest levels of value-motivation were reported. However, volunteers in Sweden and Italy showed higher and lower levels of value-motivation, respectively, than the level of social protection would predict.
2. Volunteering is a way to "signal" desirable characteristics to potential employers (Hustinx et al., 2010). *Volunteers in countries with high labor market flexibility*

5.3 Cultural and Structural Differences: Volunteer Work at the Red Cross in Europe

Table 5.1 Country characteristics

	Welfare regime	Labor market set-up		Civil society		Work organization	
	Social spending	Flexibility	Skill regime	Discontent	Citizenship	Resources	Demands
	Social protection in PPS per capita, 2008[a]	Average job tenure 2011[b]	Level of skill specificity[c]	Confidence in institutions[d]	Norm of critical citizenship[e]	Prevalence of discretion and learning[f]	Workload and mental demand[g]
Austria	8844	11.13	Industry	High	Moderate	Moderate	Moderate
France	8353	11.95	Industry	Moderate	Moderate	Moderate	Moderate
Germany	8145	11.47	Industry	High	Moderate	Moderate	Moderate
Italy	7253	12.87	Firm	Low	Moderate	Low	Low
Lithuania	2465	7.70	General	Low	Moderate	Low	High
Spain	5730	10.95	Firm	Moderate	Moderate	Low	Low
Sweden	9142	10.57	Industry	High	High	High	High
Switzerland	9264	9.73	Industry	High	Moderate	Moderate	Moderate

Sources: [a] Eurostat (2008); [b] OECD (2011); [c] Hall and Gingerich (2009), Culpepper (2007), Knell and Srholec (2006), Sippola (2009); [d] Bellucci and Memoli (2012), Zmerli et al. (2007); [e] Blom (2009), Denters et al. (2007); [f] Eurofound (2009), Gallie (2007), Parent-Thirion et al., 2007; [g] Holman (2012)

(thus, a higher number of situations in which volunteer experiences might be used to signal desirable characteristics) and a general skill regime (where general skills such as those acquired while volunteering are valued) should report higher career-related motivation than volunteers in countries with low labor market flexibility and a firm-specific skill regime. In line with this hypothesis, we found volunteers in countries with low labor market flexibility and high importance of firm-specific skills, such as Italy and Spain, to report the lowest career motivation. In turn, volunteers in Lithuania, where labor market flexibility is high, and skill specificity is low, reported the highest career motivation.

3. Volunteers are not only motivated to help people in need, i.e., volunteer for altruistic reasons, but also to address problems faced by societies and political systems, i.e., volunteer out of political responsibility (Neufeind et al., 2014). This motivation should be affected by the current situation in a country as well as dominant norms. Thus, we hypothesized that *volunteers in societies displaying high levels of citizen discontent with their government and its institutions would report a higher motivation through political responsibility than those in societies with low levels of political discontent.* Furthermore, we predicted that *volunteers in countries with a strong societal norm of critical citizenship would report higher political-responsibility motivation than those in countries with a weak societal norm of critical citizenship.* We found across the eight countries that low or medium levels of confidence, as in Lithuania or Spain, as well as a high prevalence of critical citizenship norms, as in Sweden, correlated with high political-responsibility motivation.

4. Volunteering is an activity that can compensate for deficiencies in one's paid job and substitute for what is missing in the work domain (Grant, 2012), for instance, in terms of significance or autonomy. *Volunteers in countries with low levels of discretion and learning in the workplace should report higher paid work complementation motivation than those in countries with high levels of discretion and learning in the workplace.* In line with this hypothesis, we found volunteers in Italy, Lithuania, and Spain, where discretion and learning in the workplace tend to be lower, reported the highest complementation motivation, while volunteers in Austria, France, and Sweden, where autonomy in the workplace tends to be higher, reported significantly lower complementation motivations.

5. Volunteering can function as a buffer against stress and demands of the paid work domain (Mojza & Sonnentag, 2010). Thus, *volunteers in countries with high levels of stress and demand in the workplace should report higher paid work compensation motivation than those in countries with low levels of stress and demand in the workplace.* We found some evidence for this hypothesis, as volunteers in countries with high demand, such as Lithuania and Sweden, report high work-compensation motivation. However, volunteers in Austria and France showed unexpectedly high compensation motivation, while those in Germany and Switzerland showed unexpectedly low compensation. These findings need further exploration.

In sum, our findings demonstrate that volunteering is not (only) an individual prosocial behavior but is also embedded in and determined by economic, political, and cultural contexts. While volunteering can be understood from a social-psychological perspective as "longer term, sustained prosocial behavior" (Penner et al., 2005), only by adding the perspectives of political psychology as well as work psychology can a complete picture be obtained: volunteering as a multifunctional activity that reflects individuals' environment.

5.3.1 Same Language, Similar Motives

In our cross-national study, we found language-related differences between France, Germany, and Switzerland in the motives for volunteering at the Red Cross (cf. Neufeind et al., 2015). This is remarkable, given that all volunteers are Western Europeans working for the same organization. In addition to the national differences between the three countries, however, French and German cultural characteristics also extend into the respective linguistic regions of Switzerland: The French- and German-speaking parts of Switzerland differ from each other, but at the same time resemble the motives in Germany and France, with more similar motives between France and the French-speaking part of Switzerland than between Germany and the German-speaking part of Switzerland. When all the motives are considered together, the significance of the motives in French-speaking Switzerland is more similar to that in France than to that in German-speaking Switzerland (Fig. 5.1).

5.3.2 Volunteers in Non-Profit Organizations

What are the implications of these results? For volunteers in non-profit organizations, the most important insight is certainly that, even in countries with broad structural and cultural similarities, such as France, Germany, and Switzerland, there are significant differences in motivation. Since we were able to control for the influence of the organization and the activity relatively well in our study (all volunteers worked for the Red Cross, differences between the areas of activity were statistically controlled), our results show that the importance of different motives for taking up the same volunteering activity does indeed differ between countries. For practitioners in multi- and international non-profit organizations such as the Red Cross or Amnesty International, this means that it is not possible to make a blanket assumption about "the" motives of "their" volunteers. Rather, recruitment strategies and organizational practices must take into account country-specific motives. This means that there are certain limits to the current trends toward standardization in volunteer management.

However, the findings reported in this chapter serve to discuss the current efforts of many political and third-sector actors to promote civil society. Our findings show

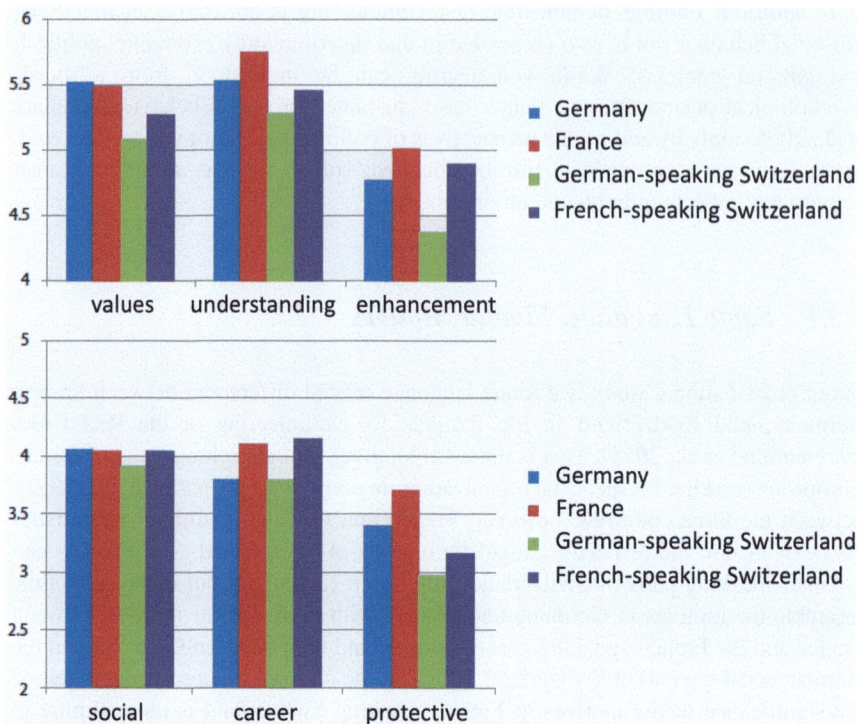

Fig. 5.1 Motivation for volunteer work in Germany, France, and Switzerland

that volunteering is not only individual prosocial behavior, but a *multifunctional* activity that is embedded in and influenced by an economic, political, and cultural context. Volunteering is not only a result of individual attitudes, but also represents a reaction to a social context. Consequently, the potential level of involvement—the potential for engagement (Gensicke, 2006)—is not universal, but rather determined by the specific social context in which volunteers are embedded. The fact that 40% of adults in Sweden are engaged in volunteer work, but less than 20% in Spain, does not necessarily mean that political and civil society actors in Spain are less good at "raising the engagement potential." Rather, structural as well as cultural factors suggest precisely these differences. However, this should not be misunderstood as determinism. Even if structural factors such as welfare state and labor market institutions are relatively rigid, cultural factors, such as values of egalitarianism and solidarity, are subject to social change. The direction in which societies are changing is also determined by civil society activities. In short, volunteering is determined by the social context, but also plays a role in determining it.

References

Bellucci, P., & Memoli, V. (2012). The determinants of democracy satisfaction in Europe. In D. Sanders, P. Magalhaes, & G. Toka (Eds.), *Citizens and the European polity: Mass attitudes towards the European and national polities* (pp. 9–38). Oxford University Press.

Blom, R. (2009). Divergent citizenship. In A. Konttinen (Ed.), *Civic mind and good citizenship*. Tampere University Press.

Cingano, F. (2003). Returns to specific skills in industrial districts. *Labour Economics, 10*(2), 149–164. https://doi.org/10.1016/S0927-5371(03)00005-8

Culpepper, P. D. (2007). Small states and skill specificity: Austria, Switzerland, and interemployer cleavages in coordinated capitalism. *Comparative Political Studies, 40*(6), 611–637. https://doi.org/10.1177/0010414006295927

Day, K. M., & Devlin, R. A. (1998). The payoff to work without pay: volunteer work as an investment in human capital. *Canadian Journal of Economics, 31*, 1179–1191.

De Tocqueville, A. (1835/2002). *Democracy in America* (H. Reeve, Transl.). The Pennsylvania State University. Online available.

Dekker, P., & Halman, L. (2003). Volunteering and values: An introduction. In P. Dekker & L. Halman (Eds.), *The values of volunteering: Cross-cultural perspectives* (pp. 1–18). Kluwer.

Denters, B., Gabriel, O., & Torcal, M. (2007). Norms of good citizenship. In J. W. V. Deth, J. R. N. Montero, & A. Westholm (Eds.), *Citizenship and involvement in European democracies*. Routledge.

Dlabac, O. (2016). Lokale Autonomie und Milizprinzip unter veränderten Vorzeichen – Neue Modelle der Gemeinde- und Schulorganisation. In M. Heinzer & J. Hangartner (Eds.), *Gemeinden in der Schul-Governance der Schweiz: Steuerungskultur im Umbruch, Educational Governance* (pp. 125–145). Springer VS.

Dlabac, O., Rohner, A., Zenger, T., & Kübler, D. (2014). *Die Milizorganisation der Gemeindeexekutivenim Kanton Aargau: Rekrutierungsprobleme und Reformvorschläge (Studienberichte des Zentrums für Demokratie Aarau Nr. 4)*. Zentrum für Demokratie Aarau.

Eurofound. (2009). *Working conditions in the European Union: Work organisation*. Office for Official Publications of the European Communities.

Eurostat. (2008). *Eurostat*. http://epp.eurostat.ec.europa.eu/

Finkelstein, M. A. (2011). Correlates of individualism and collectivism: Predicting volunteer activity. *Social Behavior and Personality, 39*(5), 597–606.

Freeman, R. B. (1997). Working for nothing: The supply of volunteer labor. *Journal of Labor Economics, 15*(1), 140–166.

Freitag, M., Bundi, P., & Flick Witzig, M. (2019). *Milizarbeit in der Schweiz. Zahlen und Fakten zum politischen Leben in der Gemeinde*. NZZ Libro.

Gallie, D. (2007). Production regimes and the quality of employment in Europe. *Annual Review of Sociology, 33*, 85–104.

Gensicke, T. (2006). Zusammenfassung. In T. Gensicke, S. Picot, & S. Geiss (Eds.), *Freiwilliges Engagement in Deutschland 1999–2004* (pp. 13–33). Verlag für Sozialwissenschaften.

Geser, H. (1987). Historische und aktuelle Aspekte nebenamtlicher Politik und Verwaltung in Schweizer Gemeinden. In H. Geser, P. Farago, R. Fluder, & E. Gräub (Eds.), *Gemeindepolitik zwischen Milizorganisation und Berufsverwaltung: Vergleichende Untersuchungen in 223 deutschschweizer Gemeinden* (pp. 16–33). Haupt.

Grant, A. M. (2012). Giving time, time after time: Work design and sustained employee participation in corporate volunteering. *Academy of Management Review, 37*, 589–615.

Grönlund, H., Holmes, K., Kang, C., Cnaan, R., Handy, F., Brudney, J., Haski-Leventhal, D., Hustinx, L., Kassam, M., Meijs, L. C. P. M., Pessi, A. B., Ranade, B., Smith, K. A., Yamauchi, N., & Zrinščak, S. (2011). Cultural values and volunteering: A cross-cultural comparison of students' motivation to volunteer in 13 countries. *Journal of Academic Ethics, 9*(2), 87–106.

Hall, P. A., & Gingerich, D. W. (2009). Varieties of capitalism and institutional complementarities in the political economy: An empirical analysis. *British Journal of Political Science, 39*(3), 449–482.

Handy, F., Cnaan, R. A., Hustinx, L., Kang, C., Brudney, J. L., Haski-Leventhal, D., Holmes, K., Meijs, L. C. P. M., Pessi, A. B., Ranade, B., Yamauchi, N., & Zrinscak, S. (2010). A cross-cultural examination of student volunteering: Is it all about résumé building? *Nonprofit and Voluntary Sector Quarterly, 39*(3), 498–523.

Hodgkinson, V. A. (2003). Volunteering in global perspective. In P. Dekker & L. Halman (Eds.), *The values of volunteering* (pp. 35–53). Springer.

Hoelscher, M. (2012). Spielarten des Kapitalismus und Kompetenzen von Hochschulabsolventinnen und -absolventen. *Kölner Zeitschrift für Soziologie und Sozialpsychologie, 64*(3), 479–505.

Hofstede, G. (2001). *Culture's consequences: Comparing values, behaviors, institutions and organizations across nations*. Sage.

Holman, D. (2012). Job types and job quality in Europe. *Human Relations, 66*(4), 475–502.

Hustinx, L., Handy, F., Cnaan, R. A., Brudney, J. L., Pessi, A. B., & Yamauchi, N. (2010). Social and cultural origins of motivations to volunteer: A comparison of university students in six countries. *International Sociology, 25*(3), 349–382. https://journals.sagepub.com/doi/10.11 77/0268580909360297

Hwang, M., Grabb, E., & Curtis, J. (2005). Why get involved? Reasons for voluntary-association activity among Americans and Canadians. *Nonprofit and Voluntary Sector Quarterly, 34*(3), 387–403.

Katz, E., & Rosenberg, J. (2005). An economic interpretation of institutional volunteering. *European Journal of Political Economy, 21*(2), 429–443.

Ketterer, H., Güntert, S. T., Oostlander, J., & Wehner, T. (2015). Das "Schweizer Milizsystem". In T. Wehner & S. T. Güntert (Eds.), *Psychologie der Freiwilligenarbeit* (pp. 221–246). Springer.

Knell, M., & Srholec, M. (2006). *Emerging varieties of capitalism in central and Eastern Europe: Varieties of capitalism in post-communist countries*. Palgrave.

Kriesi, H., & Trechsel, A. H. (2008). *The politics of Switzerland: Continuity and change in a consensus democracy*. Cambridge University Press.

Kussau, J., Güntert, S. T., Oertel, L., & Wehner, T. (2007). Milizsystem zwischen Freiwilligkeit und Erwerbsarbeit. *Zürcher Beiträge zur Psychologie der Arbeit, 1*.

Kussau, J., & Wehner, T. (2007, September 10). Eine Milizbehörde am Scheideweg. Zur Freiwilligentätigkeit in der Schulpflege am Beispiel des Kantons Zürich. *Neue Zürcher Zeitung*.

Ladner, A. (2015). Die Abhängigkeit der Gemeinden von der Milizpolitik. In S. Bütikofer, A. Müller, & A. Suisse (Eds.), *Bürgerstaat und Staatsbürger. Milizpolitik zwischen Mythos und Moderne* (pp. 105–123). NZZ Verlag.

Ladner, A., Steiner, R., Horber-Papazian, K., Fiechter, J., Jacot-Descombes, C., & Kaiser, C. (2013). *Gemeindemonitoring 2009/2010. Bericht der fünften gesamtschweizerischen Gemeindeschreiberbefragung (KPM-Schriftenreihe Nr. 48)*. KPM-Verlag.

Menchik, P. L., & Weisbrod, B. A. (1987). Volunteer labor supply. *Journal of Public Economics, 32*(2), 159–183.

Mojza, E. J., & Sonnentag, S. (2010). Does volunteer work during leisure time buffer negative effects of job stressors? *European Journal of Work and Organizational Psychology, 19*(2), 231–252. https://doi.org/10.1080/13594320902986097

Müller, A. (2013). *Ein Bürgerdienst für alle. Der freiwillige Einsatz im Milizsystem wird immer unbeliebter. Was tun?* https://www.avenir-suisse.ch/ein-burgerdienst-fur-alle/

Neufeind, M. (2013). *Volunteering: Exploring activities at the interface of work, leisure, and civic engagement* [PhD Thesis at ETH Zurich].

Neufeind, M., Jiranek, P., & Wehner, T. (2014). Beyond skills and structure: Justice dispositions as antecedents of young citizens' volunteering and political participation. *Journal of Community & Applied Social Psychology, 24*(4), 278–295. https://onlinelibrary.wiley.com/doi/abs/10.1002/casp.2166

References

Neufeind, M., Ketterer, H., & Wehner, T. (2015). Der Einfluss struktureller und kultureller Faktoren auf die Motivation Freiwilliger – ein Ländervergleich. In T. Wehner & S. T. Güntert (Eds.), *Psychologie der Freiwilligenarbeit* (pp. 265–279). Springer.

OECD. (2011). *OECD.Stat*. http://stats.oecd.org/

Parent-Thirion, A., Fernández Macías, E., Hurley, J., & Vermeylen, G. (2007). *Fourth European working conditions survey*. European Foundation for the Improvement of Living and Working Conditions.

Penner, L. A., Dovidio, J. F., Piliavin, J. A., & Schroeder, D. A. (2005). Prosocial behavior: Multilevel perspectives. *Annual Review of Psychology, 56*, 365–392.

Prouteau, L., & Wolff, F.-C. (2006). Does volunteer work pay off in the labor market? *The Journal of Socio-Economics, 35*(6), 992–1013.

Rubery, J., & Grimshaw, D. (2003). *The organization of employment: An international perspective*. Palgrave Macmillan.

Salamon, L. M., & Anheier, H. (1998). Social origins of civil society: Explaining the nonprofit sector cross-nationally. *VOLUNTAS: International Journal of Voluntary and Nonprofit Organizations, 9*(3), 213–248. https://doi.org/10.1023/a:1022058200985

Schwartz, S. H. (1994). Beyond individualism/collectivism: New cultural dimensions of values. In U. Kim, H. C. Triandis, C. Kagitcibasi, S.-C. Choi, & G. Yom (Eds.), *Individualism and collectivism: Theory, method and application*. Sage.

Schwartz, S. H. (1999). A theory of cultural values and some implications for work. *Applied Psychology: An International Review, 48*(1), 23–47.

Sippola, M. (2009). The two faces of Nordic management? Nordic firms and their employee relations in the Baltic States. *The International Journal of Human Resource Management, 20*(9), 1929–1944. https://doi.org/10.1080/09585190903142381

Spence, M. (1973). Job market signaling. *The Quarterly Journal of Economics, 87*(3), 355–374.

Strauß, S. (2009). Ehrenamt in Deutschland und Großbritannien: Sprungbrett zurück auf den Arbeitsmarkt? *Kölner Zeitschrift für Soziologie und Sozialpsychologie, 61*(4), 647–670.

Ziemek, S. (2006). Economic analysis of volunteers' motivations: A cross-country study. *Journal of Socio-Economics, 53*(3), 532–555.

Zmerli, S., Newton, K., & Montero, J. R. (2007). Trust in people, confidence in political institutions, and satisfaction with democracy. In J. W. Van Deth, J. R. Montero, & A. Westholm (Eds.), *Citizenship and involvement in European democracies: A comparative analysis* (pp. 35–65). Routledge.

Open Access This chapter is licensed under the terms of the Creative Commons Attribution 4.0 International License (http://creativecommons.org/licenses/by/4.0/), which permits use, sharing, adaptation, distribution and reproduction in any medium or format, as long as you give appropriate credit to the original author(s) and the source, provide a link to the Creative Commons license and indicate if changes were made.

The images or other third party material in this chapter are included in the chapter's Creative Commons license, unless indicated otherwise in a credit line to the material. If material is not included in the chapter's Creative Commons license and your intended use is not permitted by statutory regulation or exceeds the permitted use, you will need to obtain permission directly from the copyright holder.

Chapter 6
Practical Implications

We close our book with some practical implications. On the one hand, we look specifically at the conditions for sustained volunteering, and on the other hand, we derive some general practical implications from an organizational psychology perspective.

6.1 Which Design Features Influence Sustained Engagement?

What characteristics ensure that volunteers identify with the NPO (non-profit organization), are satisfied and willing to work, or are committed to the NPO's concerns? (cf. van Schie et al., 2015).

6.1.1 General Satisfaction

Interestingly, volunteer satisfaction is best predicted by good information flow within an organization. It is also important to present volunteers with a variety of tasks and to have in place a volunteer coordinator who can support volunteers' autonomy. Therefore, if an organization wants its volunteers to feel satisfied with their work, it is important, first and foremost, to ensure that relevant information is freely available to all and that it is disseminated. Furthermore, volunteer tasks should be as varied as possible, while coordinators should be interested in their volunteers' ideas, express confidence in their skills, and encourage them to be independent.

6.1.2 Joy of Work

Compared to general satisfaction, which is primarily influenced by organizational factors such as the flow of information or coordination, the tasks themselves become more important in terms of job satisfaction. In order to experience liveliness, devotion, and absorption during volunteer work, it is necessary above all to have varied tasks whose importance is clearly evident. A third influencing factor, which is rather out of reach of an NPO, is recognition by the private environment. Therefore, if volunteers feel that friends, family, and acquaintances value their voluntary work, they also show more enthusiasm for that work. Although the NPO can hardly influence the level of recognition experienced in the private sphere, the findings could still be taken into account in symbolic forms of recognition (e.g., in "thank-you" events). Overall, it is clear that an NPO promotes committed volunteers if it pays particular attention to diverse and significant tasks.

6.1.3 Identification with the Organization

Identification with an organization is largely influenced by a match of values between volunteers and the respective NPO. Volunteers will better identify with an organization if they believe that both parties aspire to the same values. The second and third most important factors are the diversity of tasks and recognition from the private sector. Overall, identification with the NPO can be particularly encouraged if its values are clearly recognizable (e.g., in its strategy, recruitment processes, or communication) and if they correspond to the values of its volunteers, if the tasks are varied, and the private environment is taken into account in the recognition process.

6.1.4 Organizational Commitment

As with identification, for organizational commitment the congruence of values is once again the strongest design feature. In addition, recognition by the organization's employees also has a strong influence. This finding shows that an appreciative working atmosphere with employed (i.e., non-voluntary) colleagues is able to promote volunteers' concrete willingness to act for organizational concerns. Decision-making autonomy in tasks can also promote this willingness. If the NPO wants volunteers to work not only for the beneficiaries of their programs but also for the organization itself, it should ensure that their values are consistent. In addition, recognition by the salaried workforce, and decision-making autonomy in tasks, can help to strengthen volunteers' willingness to perform organizational tasks.

6.2 Summary from the Perspective of Industrial and Organizational Psychology, with Recommendations for Action

In this book, we presented concepts of work and organizational psychology in order to enrich volunteer research, which to date has largely focused on individual motivations and the personal development of volunteers with an activity perspective. The concepts presented herein illuminate the tasks and point out relevant aspects of the organizational context. Our survey findings clearly showed that successful task design and the organizational context are important not only for gainful employment but also for volunteer work.

Sustained engagement can be promoted by motivating tasks, support for autonomy, congruence of values, transparent communication within the organization, and by recognition.

Good organizational conditions (such as a good flow of information or coordination that supports autonomy) tend to promote the general satisfaction of volunteers, while motivating work tasks particularly promote job satisfaction. In contrast, identification with the organization and organizational commitment is strongly determined by the perceived matching of values. The importance of individual design features therefore differs significantly depending on the goal being pursued. The findings of our studies (see Chap. 3) illustrate that the indicators of sustained engagement in volunteer work are also predicted differently from the characteristics of the tasks and the organization.

Individual indicators of sustained volunteerism can be supported in a targeted manner: General satisfaction is particularly supported by organizational framework conditions, and joy of work comes through diverse and significant tasks. Identification with and commitment to the NPO are particularly promoted through congruence of values and recognition by employees.

What can NPOs actually do to meet the challenges of coordinating volunteers? Although a content-related analysis of local conditions is always advisable to determine at which points the optimization of design features seems sensible and necessary, we derive some general practical recommendations for action:

- The tasks assigned to volunteers should be as *varied and meaningful* (to others) as possible, in order to promote the joy of work. The assignment of highly varied tasks/workload has particularly high potential because this characteristic is currently the least common but yet is extremely important, both for satisfaction and joy of work as well as for identification with the organization. Thus, a variety of tasks can be supported by means of systematic task and job changes.
- Coordinators should support the *autonomy of volunteers* by encouraging volunteers to ask questions about the organization and its activities, giving them confidence in their abilities and showing interest in their values. In addition, coordinators should communicate the organizational issues in an understandable

and insightful way so that volunteers can take seriously and fulfill their role as representatives of the organization.
- In order to enable congruence of values between an NPO and its volunteers, the NPO's *values should be clearly communicated* in its organizational strategy, made visible and responsive in mutual exchange, and, if possible, already taken into account when recruiting volunteers.
- *Employee recognition* could be improved in many projects, for example, by conducting feedback discussions or establishing exchange forums. However, it is essential that employee recognition is communicated without a binding character. In addition, an attempt can be made to acknowledge the positive effects of recognition from the private sphere by incorporating this source within the NPO's communications.

As our book has shown, methods of work and organizational psychology not only have an impact in gainful employment, but should also be considered in the context of volunteer work. Anyone who wants to promote sustained engagement among volunteers must not rely on appeals to "good citizens and fellow human beings," but must instead invest in good task design and competent support.

The past few years have brought several crises, including the refugee crisis that started in 2015 and then the COVID-19 pandemic that started in 2020. Each time, we saw how crisis also necessitated and motivated the use of volunteers. From the experiences and research of past years, two points became clear, to which we should pay more attention in the future:

1. Volunteering is more dependent on the *social context* than was previously observed. Some citizens, especially those who were not previously involved, experienced internal conflict and tensions with other actors: What do I, my family, and others think about refugee policy or the pandemic? People act upon what they think *their* social context expects them to do or think.
2. *Concepts of justice* play a decisive role. This must include not only the recipients of aid and those who perform voluntary work, but also those who are not committed. Concepts of justice differ significantly between committed and non-committed individuals (cf. Strubel & Kals, 2018): Is it fair to help refugees or support government action to fight the COVID-19 pandemic? Some agree whereas others would take the opposite perspective.

Practice needs research; research needs practice: This is the conclusion of our scientific work.

References

Strubel, I. T., & Kals, E. (2018). Scope of justice and voluntary work in refugee aid. *Conflict Dynamics, 7*(1), 40–49.

References

van Schie, S., Güntert, S. T., Oostlander, J., & Wehner, T. (2015). How the organizational context impacts volunteers. *VOLUNTAS: International Journal of Voluntary and Nonprofit Organizations, 26*, 1570–1590.

Open Access This chapter is licensed under the terms of the Creative Commons Attribution 4.0 International License (http://creativecommons.org/licenses/by/4.0/), which permits use, sharing, adaptation, distribution and reproduction in any medium or format, as long as you give appropriate credit to the original author(s) and the source, provide a link to the Creative Commons license and indicate if changes were made.

The images or other third party material in this chapter are included in the chapter's Creative Commons license, unless indicated otherwise in a credit line to the material. If material is not included in the chapter's Creative Commons license and your intended use is not permitted by statutory regulation or exceeds the permitted use, you will need to obtain permission directly from the copyright holder.

The manufacturer's authorised representative in the EU is Springer Nature Customer Service Centre GmbH, Europaplatz 3, 69115 Heidelberg, Germany. If you have any concerns regarding our products, please contact ProductSafety@springernature.com

Printed and bound by CPI Group (UK) Ltd, Croydon, CR0 4YY
23/03/2026
02076446-0009